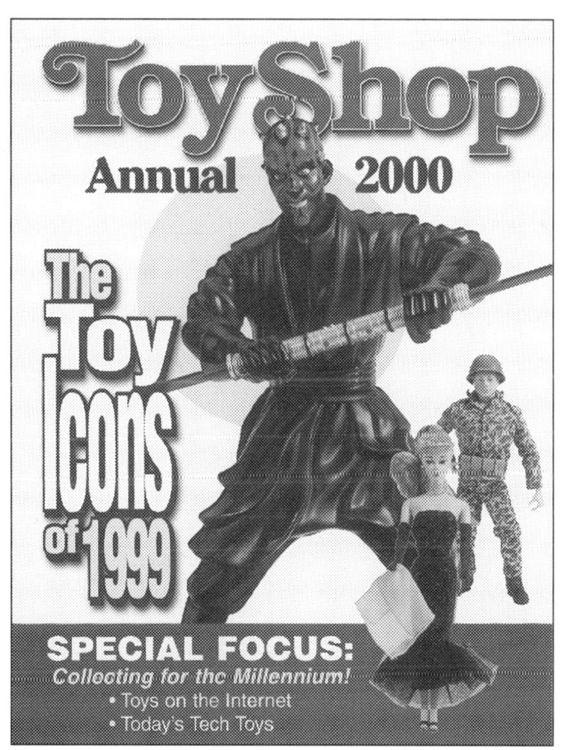

Toy Shop Annual 2000

Table of Contents

Foreword

This annual directory is one we're proud of. We have some timely stories about our hobby plus directories of clubs, dealers, manufacturers and toy shows that will make you want to hang on to this annual and refer to it often in the year 2000.

While 1999 was a difficult year for many in the toy hobby, we at *Toy Shop* and Krause Publications are also proud of some of the moves we made to further solidify our force in the collecting hobby (*see page 34*).

Pictured on our cover are Solo in the Spotlight Barbie, a repro-duction of a vintage Barbie fashion from the 1960s; 1960s G.I. Joe soldier; and Thinkway's Darth Maul interactive bank from 1999. On our back cover are McFarlane Toys' Austin Powers action figures.

Thanks to Ross Hubbard, Kris Kandler and Tom Dupuis for cover photography and design; Editor Sharon Korbeck; and the advertising staff of *Toy Shop* magazine, all of whom were essential parts of publishing this book.

Mike Jacquart
jacquartm@krause.com

Toy Shop Annual 2000

Editor: Sharon Korbeck (korbecks@krause.com)
Associate Editor: Mike Jacquart (jacquartm@krause.com)
Cover design by Tom Dupuis
Visit us online at www.krause.com or www.toyshopmag.com

Advertiser Index

E-Collecting

Shows, Magazines Feel Internet Collecting Squeeze

By Sharon Korbeck

Have you fallen victim to the "dot.com" disease?

Do you begin every phrase with the prefix "e-"?

Is your communication limited to keyboard chats rather than coffee breaks?

If so, you, like a growing number of other collectors, may have been romanced by the lure of Internet collecting, buying and selling — collectively known as e-commerce.

It's hard to recall a year as Internet-glutted and e-commerce pervasive as 1999. *Time* magazine named Amazon.com's CEO Jeff Bezos the most influential person in technology. Venerable auction houses like Sotheby's and Butterfield & Butterfield teamed up with Internet powerhouses Amazon.com and eBay, respectively. Even Martha Stewart took her stylish empire public.

So it isn't surprising that even mom and pop dealers in antiques, toys and even garage sale rejects are finding the Internet an alternative way to conduct sales.

That changing marketplace has created waves in the industry as tumultuous as Hurricane Floyd. Longtime dealers are dabbling in cyber waters. The audience for collectibles has expanded. The gavels have been raised; let the bidding begin.

The rationale for entering the golden e-ring is simple — a vastly expanded marketplace means more potential buyers . . . millions more.

That means that those previously unable to attend a Sotheby's auction to bid on 18th-century furniture can do so via cyberspace. Respected auction houses authenticate their wares, offering customer service smaller auction sites and dealers cannot.

That's right. Even higher-end collectibles like furniture, jewelry and celebrity memorabilia have joined Barbie dolls, Beanie Babies and board games on e-commerce auction and buy/sell sites.

With the advent and rise of the Internet, collectors are either jumping in headfirst . . . or shyly testing the waters. For toy shows and toy magazines, even for some wavering collectors, the Internet poses an interesting, yet frightening and realistic question.

What will happen when everyone is collecting online? Will the magazines die off? Will toy shows become extinct? Will bricks and mortar toy stores become barren warehouses?

Conventional wisdom says the Internet will thrive in the domain of e-commerce. Fledgling companies are joining the ranks of the "dot.coms," often not turning profits but making big news and large stock returns.

But that does not have to mean the end of conventional collecting or toy buying as we know it.

Toy Shop columnist Mark Rich has been following the Internet collecting craze. Of the phenomenon he commented, "Countless collectors lead busy lives that leave little time for the task of Internet searching.

"Where will they turn? They turn to whatever venue can bring them information about the toys they desire and do so with the least work and the most pleasure. The sellers who can figure out how to do that will be the next leaders in the toy collecting field."

Those other venues include toy shows and toy publications.

"I do believe a new equilibrium will be reached, one in which the toy shows, toy magazines and online auctions co-exist. They may even grow to depend upon one another," he added.

The future of online collecting and e-commerce may become more clear and well-defined in the 21st century. It may be that a healthy mix of community, commerce and collecting will take the industry in places it likely has never seen before.

Sharon Korbeck is editor of "Toy Shop" magazine. Part of the commentary in this article was taken from a two-part story on collecting on the Internet, written by Mark Rich. His comments originally ran in "Toy Shop" magazine.

Krause Publications can be accessed online at www.krause.com. The company's online auction site is located at www.collectit.net.

Krause Publications' latest venture into the Internet world is cooperation with eBay the auction site as publisher of "eBay magazine."

> **"I do believe a new equilibrium will be reached, one in which the toy shows, toy magazines and online auctions co-exist. They may even grow to depend upon one another."**
>
> *Mark Rich,*
> *"Toy Shop" columnist*

Pokémon vs. Jar Jar

Japanese Craze Gives 'Episode I' Short Shelf Life

Hasbro's Pokémon characters were the crown princes of toys in 1999.

By Sharon Korbeck

In early 1999, a gangly Gungan named Jar Jar Binks was supposed to storm the world as the comic relief in *Star Wars Episode I: The Phantom Menace.*

Jar Jar's intensely annoying on-screen antics and gobbledygook speech, however, fell far short of many adult filmgoers' expectations.

Oh, the film still fared well and George Lucas's reign is safe. After all the hype, *Episode I,* the film, may have succeeded. But in the toy world, the hype soon faded and store shelves were glutted with Jar Jar spin-pops and inflatable chairs and Jabba the Hutt slime.

There was "the initial throng of people," said Samantha Ross, a Toys R Us supervisor in Jacksonville, Fla.

"The core toys still did well," Ross said, but things cooled off pretty quickly, she added.

Ross said her store's Episode I area was slated to stay up until Christmas, but it was taken down early.

"It [Pokémon] spans boys and girls. That's what's making it a phenomenon."

— Samantha Ross
Toys R Us supervisor

What happened? How could product based on a surefire, much-anticipated film like *Star Wars* remain sluggish?

Some point to overproduction of the toys. Earlier this year, *Toy Shop* reported that Hasbro spent over $600 million and offered 7.5 percent of its company equity to Lucasfilm for a nine-year *Star Wars* deal. But by mid-1999, however, Hasbro reported that they expected sales to reach only $600 million in 1999 — as much as $200 million lower than expected.

Meanwhile, PepsiCo, which focused its $2 billion Star Wars efforts on its Taco Bell, Pizza Hut and KFC restaurants, reportedly had not seen additional traffic generated by the tie-in toys.

What did fare well in toyland for *Star Wars,* however, was LEGO's *Episode I* sets. Within the first five weeks of sales, the toy set a new record for LEGO sales in a one-month period.

Episode I, by some accounts, failed to appeal to children. That may have been its bane at the toy store.

According to Thomas Alfonsie, K-

B Toys head of merchandising, "The only way for [*Star Wars* toys] to be a real long-term success is to get the kids."

So, while some *Episode I* toys (like the 12-inch Darth Maul figure by Hasbro) did well with collectors, what did "get the kids"?

A Japanese menagerie of alternately cute and freaky critters known as Pocket Monsters or Pokémon. Pokémon's first incarnation was a Japanese video game, issued by Nintendo in 1996. The red and blue versions of the Game Boy reached the U.S. in 1998; that same year, the trading card game by Wizards of the Coast really started to take off. By summer 1999, few kids didn't know who Pikachu, Blastoise and Charizard were.

The Pokémon craze had hit toy stores. Early in the year, "we could tell it was going to pick up," Ross said. And it was Christmas, 1999's anticipated best-seller.

What does Pokémon have that *Episode I* apparently didn't? "It spans boys and girls. That's what's making it a phenomenon," according to Ross.

"It's got the possibility of being bigger than *Episode I*," Ross predicted.

In later 1999, Hasbro, maker of the majority of Pokémon toys, purchased Wizards of the Coast, placing the white-hot trading card game under its

McFarlane Toys sailed high with impeccable likenesses of John, Paul, George and Ringo from "Yellow Submarine." The revival of the animated 1960s Beatles film led to increased interest in the collectibles by McFarlane, Corgi and more.

corporate umbrella.

The move was hoped to strengthen Hasbro's already tight grip on the games industry, adding the power hobby store distribution.

So by the end of 1999, Pokémon was poised as the toy to cause the most holiday toy aisle crushes. But what about the first half of the year?

Films Fill Toy Aisles

After *Episode I* died down in theaters, it was time for the second-biggest film property to make its shagadelic debut.

Austin Powers: The Spy Who Shagged Me fared much better in theaters than its prequel. It's groovy fashions and snappy dialogue influenced many toys and collectibles. Talking figures from Trendmasters and McFarlane Toys were among the best of the bunch.

Collectors and fans of the film snatched up the trendy toys; their graphic language ("Do I make you horny?") upset some parents.

A second McFarlane almost-guaranteed success was expected at the end of the year with the late release of figures based on The Beatles' 1960s *Yellow Submarine* film.

But the film poised to give Poké-

Thinkway Toys is known for interactive toys. Pair that success with Disney/Pixar's late 1999 film "Toy Story 2," and the toys come to life! Pictured are interactive Buzz Lightyear and Woody.

mon toys a run for their money at Christmas was *Toy Story 2* — Disney/Pixar's animated sequel. Buzz and Woody return with — guess who? — as a guest star, Barbie! Woody returns as as collectible (how appropriate!), and several new characters debut. Licensed toys are slated from Mattel.

Ross said Toys R Us would feature *Toy Story 2* in its own "boutique," an area in the store designated to highlight "of-the-moment" toys.

Of the remaining films with related toy products, only Disney's *Tarzan* fared respectably on screen and in stores (although, once again, parental concern was voiced over Tarzan's allegedly-X-rated hand movements).

Film losers, at least in the toy aisle, included *The Mummy*; *Wild, Wild West* and *Iron Giant*.

Big Birthday Year

Unless you've been asleep, you know that 1999 was the birthday of toy giants Barbie (who turned 40) and G.I. Joe (a robust 35). Commemorative figures and dolls celebrated the toys' longevity. Toys R Us's Samantha Ross said special-edition Barbies continue to be popular. She added that while Barbies appear to sell equally well to adults and children, G.I. Joe continues to intrigue adult collectors more than children.

Among the best-selling Barbie dolls were the Harley-Davidson #3 (Barbie and Ken in leather garb), a Toys R Us exclusive. Secondary market values soared immediately.

Rock & Roll Elmo by Hasbro was an anticipated Christmas, 1999, best-seller.

Movies and McFarlane Toys were an incomparable mix in 1999. "Austin Powers, The Spy Who Shagged Me" was a licensing success for numerous toy and novelty manufacturers.

Collectors also picked up the 40th Anniversary and Millennium Princess dolls initially, but many were readily available on store shelves by year end.

G.I. Joe and Barbie remain staples at toy stores. "Barbie is always going to sell," Ross said.

Other "staples" that sell well throughout the year, according to Ross, include Monopoly, Fisher-Price Little People play sets and Hasbro's Easy-Bake Oven.

What's the Talk?

Talking toys, for the last several years, have escalated in popularity. Last year, the incessant chatter of Furbies filled toy aisles. Prior to that, it was Tickle Me Elmo.

This year, Elmo's back in a rock and roll version (along with Sesame Street comrade Ernie). Ross and other Toys R Us reps said Furbies were still pretty popular at the beginning of 1999, but by the end of 1999, there were plenty to be had on shelves. Furby Babies, a miniature version, were slated to hit store shelves in the fourth quarter of 1999.

Among the other popular talking toys of 1999 were Austin Powers figures and key chains and World Wrestling Federation (WWF) figures.

Diehard Die-Cast

Die-cast vehicles, many as inexpensive as 79 cents, kept store stockers busy in 1999.

A surge in activity began in 1998 with the 50th anniversary of NASCAR. Almost every manufacturer jumped on that license; among the biggest sellers were Racing Champions and Winner's Circle items.

Ross said, however, that by early to mid-1999, "The NASCAR stuff has seemed to die down."

Mattel remained king of die-cast as owner of the Hot Wheels and Matchbox lines. Many collectors were angered at Mattel by high production numbers and lack of distribution. Whether it was Mattel's or the retailers' faults, many collectors waited until almost the end of the year to get their hands on 1999 First Edition Hot Wheels.

"We still sell a lot of the basic Hot Wheels," Ross said, adding that Mattel's Final Run has been especially popular.

Playing Mantis's Johnny Lightning die-cast has been an especially hot seller, Ross said. She said their store doesn't get many of the items in stock, but it always sells quickly.

Ready, Action!

Action figures ranging from WWF figures to Anakin Skywalker flooded store shelves in 1999. WWF, one of the hottest licenses at 1999's Toy Fair, didn't disappoint young fans wanting to nab every likeness of their favorite entertainers.

In the *Star Wars* line, the 12-inch figures (particularly Darth Maul) sold first. Thinkway's interactive talking *Star Wars* character banks were considered one of the coolest and most ingenious toys of the year by many, but some collectors and parents were hesitant to shell out $40 each. By the end of 1999, most were clearanced.

Todd McFarlane's most popular lines followed film licenses, but his Spawn line continued drawing fans, both on the primary and secondary markets.

Other action figure stand-outs came from smaller companies like 21st Century Toys (with a military line that competes with Hasbro's G.I. Joe), Toy Vault and Sideshow Toy.

What's Left?

By October, when this annual was

Disney's "Tarzan" was a huge success at the box office. Lots of Mattel's toys, however, remained clearanced on store shelves late in the year.

put together, it was still unpredictable what *the* hottest holiday toy would be. It would have been no stretch to predict that "all things Pokémon" would fare well as well as video games. Latecomers Furby Babies, Smilin' Snoopy and *Toy Story 2* toys were expected to heat up around Thanksgiving.

Ty Beanie Babies, not sold at major retail outlets, experienced somewhat of a down turn on the secondary market. But retail sales remained swift in the fourth quarter primarily due to the company's announcement that it would retire all current Beanie Babies on New Year's Eve.

A new millennium (OK, we know it *really* doesn't begin until 2001, but we're milking it anyway) may bring new, much-needed excitement to the toy industry.

The American International Toy Fair in February will announce the first toys of the new century. Will there be any surprises? Or will everything old be new again?

A young Obi-Wan Kenobi and the villainous Darth Maul were two of Hasbro's "Star Wars Episode I" action figure line.

The Best Toys of 1999

'Toy Shop' Picks its Top Toys for Collectors

It happens every year in publishing. Editors are pressed to pick the "best of" in their respective fields.

These are the days when I'm glad to be editor of a toy magazine. The research is just so much fun . . . and the ensuing play is justifiable.

Since *Toy Shop* focuses on the secondary market and the value of toys to collectors, we've used that perspective to pare our list down to the 10 best toys of the year. There's no Furby Babies or Pokémon here — we'll leave those to the kids.

Here's a look at some of 1999's greatest. We suggest picking some up if you can still find them.

1. Star Wars LEGOs, LEGO. The ubiquitous building blocks just got a little more personality, and LEGO just got a little richer with 1999's star license. The tiny Darth Maul and Qui-Gon Jinn figures are master strokes in these tiny worlds of play. We love them for their originality, play value and future collectibility. We also like to see another fine company score the Lucasfilm license.

2. Yellow Submarine action

McFarlane's Jeremy figure from the "Yellow Submarine" action figure line.

figures, McFarlane Toys. Easily the best action figure series of the year in terms of detail, execution and packaging. Master of acquiring unique and hot licenses, music fan Todd McFarlane lets nothing stand in his way. These retro-cool figures make even non-Beatles fans drool. Who would have thought this license would be fresh after 30 years?

3. Star Wars Interactive Banks, Thinkway Toys. Although some stores had reduced the price of these $40 banks by the end of the year, their charm remained. The three — Darth Maul, Qui-Gon Jinn and Obi-Wan Kenobi — could stand alone or be interlocked in a lightsaber duel. Great likenesses, haunting voices

BELOW: Living Toys' H.R. Pufnstuf figures

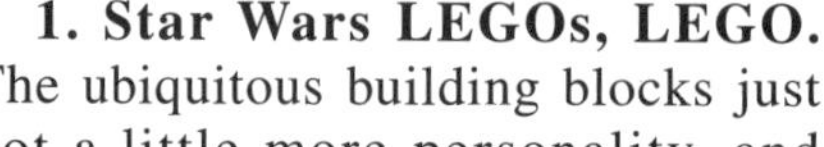

Star Wars LEGOS feature tiny, saber-wielding figures of Darth Maul and Qui-Gon Jinn.

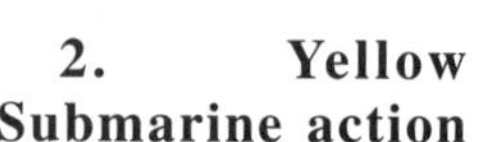

Obi-Wan Kenobi, Darth Maul and Qui-Gon Jinn do battle when connected. These interactive banks are by Thinkway Toys.

Toy Shop Annual 2000

Punk rockers Jerry Only, left, and Doyle Wolfgang Von Frankenstein, also known as The Misfits, are presented by 21st Century Toys.

Austin Powers figures by McFarlane Toys feature voice chips.

and motion-sensitive action made these banks cool and collectibles.

4. Inspector Gadget Happy Meal toy, McDonald's. Simply ingenious . . . but frustrating for parents. This multi-part oversized action figure was a creative toy when assembled, but it took many trips to the burger counter to acquire all the parts. Already selling for premium prices ($30 or more), the complete toy may be the most memorable aspect of Disney's forgettable summer 1999 film.

5. Maleficent / Captain Hook dolls, Disney Great Villains Series, Mattel. They're pure evil . . . yet purely beautiful. Barbie may have had a birthday in 1999, but these villainous dolls stole the party. Their nefarious faces, appropriate poses and fabulous packaging make them neat treats for Disney fans.

6. H.R. Pufnstuf toys, Living Toys. Thirtysomethings everywhere rejoiced when Living Toys revived these Sid and Marty Krofft Saturday morning favorites including Pufnstuf, Witchiepoo, Cling and Clang and Sigmund and the Sea Monster.

7. VW Beetle, Gate. If you couldn't afford the $19,000 new Beetle, Gate's 1:18-scale version was just as sweet. Classic rounded lines, impeccable detailing and candy colors were appreciated by admirers of the Bug.

8. Special Edition games, Parker Bros. Preparing for the

With a swashbuckling appearance, Captain Hook spices up Mattel's Great Villains series of Disney characters.

millennium was easy for Parker Brothers. It introduced special editions of several classic games. Among our top picks are Alfred Hitchcock Clue and Millennium Monopoly. Unique characters celebrated Hitchcock's 100th birthday, and special Monopoly tokens took the game into the new century.

9. Austin Powers figures, McFarlane Toys. No "groovy" references needed. These figures are dead ringers for the movie characters, and their talking bases were an added bonus.

10. The Misfits action figures, 21st Century Toys. The only thing more awesome then these figures of punk rockers Jerry Only and Doyle Wolfgang Von Frankenstein was meeting Only in person at Toy Fair. Musician action figures were rampant this year, but with their face paint, rocker garb and coffin shaped boxes, these figures hit a striking chord for both toy collectors and music fans.

"Toy Shop" magazine editorial staff Sharon Korbeck, Mike Jacquart, Elizabeth Stephan, Merry Dudley and Lisa Jacobsen contributed to this story.

Market Update
A Look at 1999's Secondary Market for Toys

By Mike Jacquart

The year 1999 will likely be remembered in the toy industry as the year *Star Wars* toys and Ty Beanie Babies cooled off, and reproduction toys heated up.

These are just some of the toys examined in this secondary market report, which also gives collectors a look at some of the top-selling toys from the late 19th century through the 1980s.

The top-10 lists were compiled from *2000 Toys & Prices*, an annual price guide book ($18.95 plus shipping) available from Krause Publications, publishers of *Toy Shop*.

Star Wars Sales Drop Off

While *Episode I* put George Lucas in the spotlight in 1999, *Star Wars* collector Chris Fawcett said the market for vintage [pre-1990] *Star*

Krause Publications' "2000 Toys & Prices" features prices on thousands of toys. Cost is $18.95. Call (800) 258-0929 to order.

Whether it's a Thinkway bank (pictured here) or another toy, Darth Maul is "the" character to collect from "Star Wars: Episode I."

Top Ten Star Wars Action Figures
(in Mint in Package condition)

1. Luke w/Telescoping Saber, Original 12, 3", 1977 . . . .$4,410
2. Jawa, Vinyl Cape, Original 12, 3", 1977 3,200
3. Anakin Skywalker, Power of the Force, 3", 1985 2,150
4. Yak Face w/coin, Power of the Force, 3", 1985 1,710
5. Boba Fett, 3", 1978 920
6. Droids, Boba Fett, 3", 1985 790
7. AT-AT Driver w/coin, Power of the Force, 3", ...660
8. IG-88, 12", 1980 640
9. Han Solo, Large Head, Original 12, 3", 1977 620
10 Early Bird Figures — Luke, Leia, R2-D2, Chewbacca, 3" 610

Wars toys has definitely cooled in the past few years.

"Prices have drifted down on the common to rare stuff," he said. "The only toys that are still going up in value are extremely perfect Mint in Box (MIB) pieces and other rare items."

Gary Morandi, a Thousand Oaks, Calif., dealer, agreed. "They're [*Star Wars* toys] not the easy sells they used to be," he said. "People are super condition conscious."

And what about the *Star Wars: Episode I* toys issued in 1999? The secondary market for *Episode I* toys was not as good as it was hoped sales would be for the first toys based on a new *Star Wars* movie in 16 years. Still, Fawcett believes the secondary market for *Episode I* toys is at least respectable.

"Nothing could match the hype, but what I've seen the market is healthy," Fawcett stated.

While there are undoubtedly plenty of Qui-Gon Jinn and Watto fans out there — and maybe even some Jar Jar Binks enthusiasts — Darth Maul is *the* guy in collecting circles.

"Maul is definitely the character to get, in any [toy] form," Fawcett said. "They're hard to find and even collec-

tors that aren't generally collecting the line have picked up Maul [action] figures."

Toy Shop action figure columnist John Marshall believes the new *Star Wars* Power of the Force figures could be sleepers down the road as collectors overlooked them in favor of *Episode I* mania.

Other Action Figures

While *Star Wars* dominated a good deal of action figure discussion in 1999, dealers said figures based on 1970s TV shows like *The Six Million Dollar Man, The Bionic Woman, Welcome Back Kotter* and *Starsky and Hutch* were among the most popular.

**The Top 10 Action Figures
(excluding Captain Action)
(in Mint in Box condition)**

1. Batgirl, Comic Heroine Posin' Dolls, Ideal, 1967 . . . .$4,500
2. Wonder Woman, Comic Heroine Posin' Dolls, Ideal, 1967 3,000
3. Supergirl, Comic Heroine Posin' Dolls, Ideal, 1967 3,000
4. Mera, Comic Heroine Posin' Dolls, Ideal, 1967 3,000
5. Scorpio, Major Matt Mason, Mattel, 1967-70 2,250
6. Batman's Wayne Foundation Penthouse, 1977 Mego, 1972-78 1,200
7. Mission Team Four-Pack, Major Matt Mason, Mattel, 1967-70 625
8. Romulan, Star Trek, Mego, 1976 600
9. Callisto, Major Matt Mason, Mattel, 1967-70 600
10. Mad Monster Castle, vinyl, Mad Monster Series, Mego 600

RIGHT: While there would likely be interest on the secondary market for a carded Kenner R2-D2 action figure from 1977 like this one, vintage [pre-1990] "Star Wars" toys are not the easy sells they used to be, dealers said. FAR RIGHT: The action figure market always seems to be strong for Mego superheroes like this 8-inch Catwoman from 1973.

**Top Ten 'Star Wars' Toys
(in Mint in Package condition)**

1. TIE Bomber, Die-Cast, 1979 . . . .$830
2. Tatooine Skiff, Power of the Force 670
3. Cantina Adventure Set, Sears Exclusive, 1977 640
4. Jawa Sand Crawler, battery-operated, 1977 610
5. Sonic Land Speeder, JC Penney Exclusive, 1977 580
6. A-Wing Fighter, Droids Box, 1983 580
7. 63rd Coin, lightsaber, Kenner, 1985 500
8. Death Star Space Station, 1977 480
9. Millennium Falcon, 1982 390
10. Cloud City Play Set, Sears Exclusive, Empire Strikes Back 1981 . . .350

"Nobody ever wanted 1970s stuff, now it's in demand," said Keir Neubauer, owner of Two Guys Toys in New Jersey. "Anything with a TV tie-in is hot, even *Emergency*."

And increased demand has led to increased prices.

Neubauer said Mego *Welcome Back Kotter* and *Starsky and Hutch* figures that only brought $20 several years ago command $50 today.

Ken Laurence, owner of Heroes Unlimited in New Jersey, has seen prices shoot up in recent years for Kenner *Six Million Dollar Man* and *The Bionic Woman* figures. Figures that sold for $75 to $100 MIB now bring $150 or more. Third issue (the last series produced) *Six Million Dollar Man* figures are especially popular, Laurence said.

"You would have paid $100 [MIB]

Interest — and prices — increased in 1999 for action figures based on 1970s TV shows like "The Bionic Woman."

ABOVE: Mattel's Big Jim line — especially European exclusives that can bring $200 in Mint in Box condition (not this figure) — were good sellers in 1999. BELOW: Marx's Best of the West, a long-neglected line, grabbed additional interest among collectors in 1999.

The Top 10 Mechanical Banks
(in Excellent condition)

1. Mikado, Kyser & Rex, 1886 . . . .$55,000
2. Jonah and the Whale, Jonah Emerges, Stevens, J.& E., 1880s 55,000
3. Rollerskating Bank, Kyser & Rex, 1880s 45,000
4. Girl Skipping Rope, Stevens, J.& E., 1890 45,000
5. Circus Bank, Shepard Hardware, 1888 45,000
6. Calamity, Stevens, J.& E., 1905 35,000
7. Harlequin, Stevens, J.& E., 1907 .22,000
8. Turtle Bank, Kilgore, 1920s 20,000
9. Picture Gallery Bank, Shepard Hardware, 1885 20,000
10. Motor Bank, Kyser & Rex, 1889. .20,000

The Top 10 G.I. Joe Figures / Sets
(All Hasbro, Mint in Package condition)

1. Foreign Soldiers of the World, Action Soldiers of the World, 1968 . . . .$5,000
2. G.I. Nurse, Action Girl Series, 1967 .4,000
3. Canadian Mountie Set, Action Soldier Series, 1967 4,000
4. Dress Parade Adventure Pack, Action Soldier Series, 1968 3,500
5. Crash Crew Fire Truck Set, Action Pilot Series, 1967 3,500
6. Talking Landing Signal Officer Set, Action Sailor Series, 1968 3,500
7. Talking Shore Patrol Set, Action Sailor Series, 1968 3,500
8. Adventure Pack, Army Bivouac Series, Action Soldier Series, 1968 3,500
9. Military Police Uniform Set, Action Soldier Series, 1967 3,500
10. Shore Patrol, Action Sailor Series, 1967 3,500

Tin toys like this Marx Milton Berle Crazy Car from the 1950s ($595 Mint) are always in demand, but they are becoming increasingly difficult to find in pristine condition.

The Top 10 Character Collectibles
(in Mint condition)

1. Superman Member Ring, 1940 . . . .$100,000
2. Action Comics #1, DC Comics, 1938, first appearance of Superman 100,000
3. Superman Gum Ring, Gum Inc., 1940 40,000
4. Little Orphan Annie Altascope Ring, Quaker, 1942 25,000
5. Superman Candy Ring, Leader Novelty Candy, 1940 22,000
6. Donald Duck Bicycle, Shelby, 1949 10,000
7. Superman-Tim Club Ring, 1940s 10,000
8. Superman Trading Cards, Gum Inc., 1940 10,000
9. Patch, 1939 10,000
10. Batman Play Set, Ideal, 1966 10,000

The Top 10 Restaurant Premiums
(in Mint condition)

1. Big Boy Nodder, Big Boy, 1960s $1,500
2. Black History, McDonald's, sold in six Detroit stores, 1988 500
3. Big Boy Bank, Large, Big Boy, 1960s 300
4. Metrozoo Happy Meal, McDonald's, distributed only in south Florida area, 1987 250
5. High Flying Kite Happy Meal, McDonald's distributed in New England area, 1986 225
6. Big Boy Bank, Medium, Big Boy, 1960s 165
7. Colonel Sanders Nodder, Kentucky Fried Chicken, 1960s 150
8. Transformers/My Little Pony, McDonald's distributed in St. Louis, Missouri area, 1985 140
9. Barbie/Hot Wheels, McDonald's distributed in Savanah, Ga., 1990 125
10. Big Boy Board Game, Big Boy, 1960s 120

RIGHT: *While toys featuring Western legends such as Roy Rogers, Hopalong Cassidy and Gene Autry have long been popular with collectors, items from 1950s and 1960s TV Westerns, like this "Wanted: Dead Or Alive" gun and holster set, are also catching on with toy fans.*

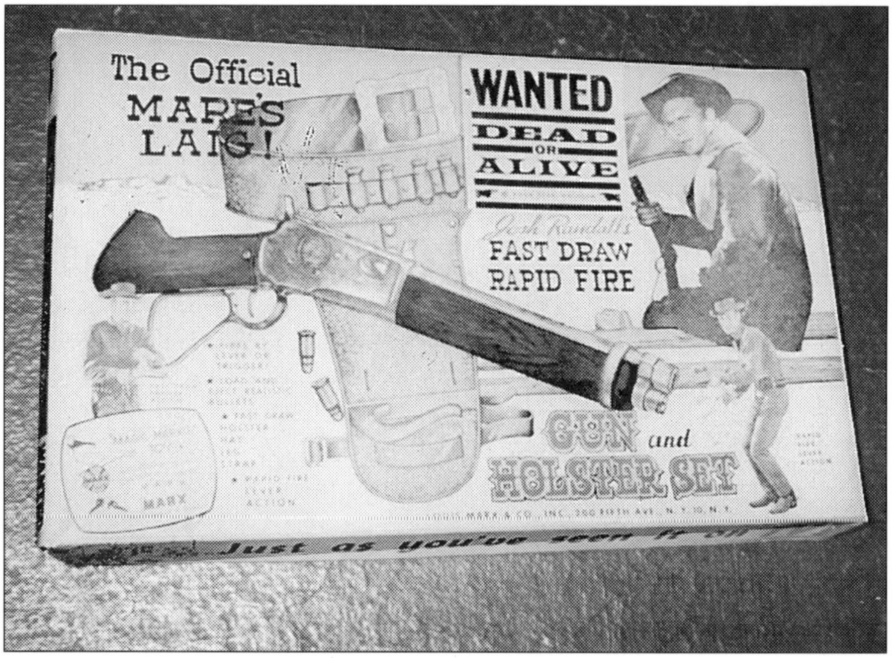

several years ago. Now it can sell for $400," he stated.

Why the interest in a decade considered forgettable by some? "These were the shows they [collectors] watched when they were kids," Laurence said.

Timothy Welsh, a noted Captain Action dealer, said Playing Mantis' decision to reissue Captain Action figures has fueled an increase in the market, "putting collectors on the hunt for all the outfits which probably won't be reissued."

Prices have remained high for most original Captain Action figures and accessories, he said, "especially those in high grade condition, can fetch some pretty outstanding prices."

Figures and dolls from the 1970s are also cropping up more frequently at auctions

A lot of three Hasbro *Charlie's Angels* dolls sold for $155, and three separate lots, each containing three 3-3/4-inch *Star Wars* figures from 1977, brought $285, $275 and $325, respectively, at a McMasters auction.

Other strong sellers included other, non-TV Mego figures; Captain Action; 1960s to 1970s G.I. Joe; Mattel's Big Jim, especially the P.A.C.K. line and European exclusives that can bring $200 MIB; and Gabriel Lone Ranger figures from the late 1970s and early 1980s.

The 1980s? Yep, today's collectors are young enough that collectibles from that decade are also in greater demand.

Remember Galoob's action figures based on *The A-Team*? These figures are commanding as much as $40 to $50 for carded 6-inch figures in MIB condition, Marshall stated.

"I can't believe something I avoided watching in high school is now considered vintage television," he said.

Another line long ignored except by devout fans, Marx's Best of the

West figures also grabbed additional attention with toy enthusiasts in 1999, Marshall said.

Western Toys

Speaking of the Old West, toys based on TV Westerns from the 1950s and 1960s are immensely popular, according to dealers and collectors of Western toys.

Toys from *Bonanza, The Rifleman, Wanted: Dead Or Alive* (Steve

---

The Top 10 Toy Guns / Sets
(in Mint in Box condition)

1. Man From U.N.C.L.E. THRUSH Rifle, Ideal, 1966 . . . . . .$2,500
2. Lost In Space Roto-Jet Gun Set, Mattel, 1966 2,000
3. Man From U.N.C.L.E. Attache Case, Ideal, 1965 1,500
4. Cap Gun Store Display, Nichols, 1950s 950
5. Showdown Set with Three Shootin' Shell Guns,
   Mattel, 1958 950
6. Man From U.N.C.L.E. Attache Case, Lone Star, 1966 850
7. Man From U.N.C.L.E. Napoleon Solo Gun Set, Ideal, 1965 . .800
8. Lost In Space Helmet and Gun Set, Remco, 1967 800
9. Roy Rogers Double Gun & Holster Set, Classy, 1950s 800
10. Man From U.N.C.L.E. Attache Case, Lone Star, 1966 750

The Top 10 Western Toys
(in Mint condition)

1. Hopalong Cassidy Roller Skates, Rollfast $1,000
2. Hopalong Cassidy Radio, Arvin, 1950s 600
3. Hopalong Cassidy Cap Gun, Wyandotte, 1950s 600
4. Roy Rogers Toy Chest, 1950s 550
5. Buck Jones Rangers Cowboy Suit, Yankiboy, 1930s 500
6. Hopalong Cassidy Western Series, Timpo, 1950s 475
7. Lone Ranger Record Player, Dekka, 1940s 450
8. Roy Rogers Play Set, Amsco, 1950s 440
9. Roy Rogers Alarm Clock, Ingraham, 1950s 440
10. Tom Mix Big Little Book Picture Puzzles, 1930s 425

McQueen), *Maverick* (James Garner) and *Have Gun Will Travel* (starring Richard Boone as Paladin) are among those in demand, as are Annie Oakley and Dale Evans.

"The lesser-known heroes are becoming more popular, probably because they [collectors] think they can't afford Roy [Rogers] or Gene [Autry]," said Ray Bott, a Western toy auctioneer in Salina, Kansas.

How much in demand are toys based on TV cowboys? Massachusetts dealer George Newcomb said a *Rifleman* gun set in MIB condition can bring $500 to $600, while a collector or dealer could probably "name their price" for a Johnny Yuma *Rebel* gun, "and the [*Rebel*] scatter gun is almost impossible to find," Newcomb added.

Two things are certain — generic Western toys aren't in demand, and the law of supply and demand leads to increasing prices.

With 30-to-40-year-old Mint specimens becoming harder to find, dealers like Jack Rosenthal of Oshkosh, Wis., are repairing toy guns. A repaired gun is worth 50 to 80 percent the price of a MIB toy, Rosenthal said, noting he repairs 10 to 20 guns per week.

Tin Toys

Like Western toy dealers, dealers of vintage tin toys from the 1920s to

The Top 10 Advertising Toys
(in Mint condition)

1. Quisp Bank, Quaker Oats, 1960s $850
2. Reddy Kilowatt Bobbin' Head, Reddy Comm., 1960s 450
3. Mr. Peanut Figure, Planters Peanuts, 1930s 375
4. Esky Store Display, *Esquire* Magazine, 1940s 375
5. Elsie the Cow Cookie Jar, Borden's, 1950s 350
6. Speedy Figure, Alka-Seltzer, 1963 350
7. Vegetable Man Display, Kraft, 1980 275
8. Barnum's Animal Crackers Cookie Jar, Nabisco, 1972 275
9. Vegetable Man Bank, Kraft, 1970s 275
10. Clark Bar Figure, Beatrice Foods, 1960s 275

The Top 10 PEZ Dispensers
(in Mint condition)

1. Make-A-Face (American card) $3,400
2. Elephant 3,200
3. Witch Regular 3,200
4. Make-A-Face (German card) 3,000
5. Lion's Club Lion 3,000
6. Mueslix 2,950
7. Pineapple 2,850
8. Space Trooper 2,000
9. Make-A-Face, loose 2,000
10. Bride 2,000

Funny Face mugs (and even a pitcher) featuring characters like Goofy Grape and Choo Choo Cherry are among the advertising toys collectors clamored for in 1999. Photo courtesy of Carren Kopleton.

Vinyl Charlie the Tuna figures are among desirable advertising toys. Photo courtesy of Carren Kopleton.

Didn't know that the Pillsbury Doughboy had a family? Well, he did, and his relatives are in great demand with collectors of advertising toys. Photo courtesy of Carren Kopleton.

1950s also reported that vintage tin toys are becoming tough to find in Mint condition, and that, in turn is driving up prices.

"Marx, Lehmann, Chein, Unique Art, any of the old standbys are in great demand," said Leo Rishty of Weston, Fla.

He said toys made by classic manufacturers like these are bringing "huge premiums [prices]," and because of that, prices for toys in lesser condition are increasing. In fact, Rishty voiced concern that buyers for vintage tin in pristine shape are becoming "priced out" of the market.

For instance, Rishty estimates that a Lehmann Zebra Cart Dare Devil from the 1920s has shot up in value from $255 in Good condition to $400. And the same toy that went for $650 Mint can now command $800.

Want another example? Rishty said collectors are willing to pay $650 for a Marx Dapper Dan the Jigger Porter in Good condition compared to $375 a year ago. In addition, Dapper Dan could be purchased for $950 a year ago in Mint condition, but a Mint specimen could go for a whopping $1,300 today, Rishty added.

"The good stuff is getting harder to find," agreed Tom Sage of Allentown, Pa., "which means that quality stuff is always in demand. Everyone is looking for toys in great condition."

Sage said Lehmann toys and tin-lithographed cars from the early 1900s to 1930s are selling well, as are boats from noted manufacturers such as Marklin and Bing.

Marx, Lehmann, and toys that feature comic characters like Popeye can bring hundreds to even thousands at the Baltimore, Md.-based Russ Harrington Antique Toys.

In another parallel to the Western toy hobby, restoration of tin toys is also becoming more common, but Harrington pointed out that some toys are harder to restore than others.

"Early American, non-lithographed pieces can be restored [quite] well. There are some good craftsmen out there," he said, adding that tin-lithographed items are much more difficult to refurbish.

Advertising Toys

While nostalgia drives the demand for many toys, that's especially true for advertising toys.

"You saw so many commercials based on these characters that they were drilled into your head. Who could forget them?" said Carren Kopleton, who runs the Queen's Collection in New Jersey.

"The thing is," Kopleton added, "their bright colors were supposed to attract you [in their original advertisements]. Who couldn't like all these smiling characters?"

Prices for advertising toys often run in the $100 range or less. While

The Top 10 View-Master Reel Sets
(Mint in package)

1.	It Came From Outer Space	$250
2.	House of Wax	250
3.	Munsters	200
4.	Charge at Feather River, The	150
5.	Dangerous Mission	150
6.	Devil's Canyon	150
7.	Drums of Tahiti	150
8.	Flight to Tangier	150
9.	Fort Ti	150
10.	French Line, The	150

While there are certainly plenty of Ty Beanie Baby enthusiasts around, secondary market prices for the cuddly charmers dropped dramatically in 1999. Spangle, introduced in 1999 (pictured here) came in pink and white head versions.

The Top 10 Beanbag Toys
(Prices are for items in Mint with Tag condition)

1. Peanut the Elephant, royal blue, Ty, retired 1995 .$4,500
2. Billionaire Bear, Ty 3,400
3. Punchers the Lobster, Ty, retired 1993 2,800
4. Bongo the Monkey, Ty, retired 1995 2,500
5. Cubbie (Brownie) the Bear, Ty, retired 1993 2,400
6. Derby the Horse, Ty, retired 1995 2,200
7. Quackers the Duck, Ty, retired 1995 2,000
8. Slither the Snake, Ty, retired 1995 2,000
9. Humphrey the Camel, Ty, retired 1995 2,000
10. Chilly the Polar Bear, Ty, retired 1994 1,850

that's not necessarily good news for dealers who believe their products are worth more than they're turning up for online, the market, conversely, is a good one for collectors looking for inexpensive, bright, cheery collectibles based on childhood characters.

Online auctions have revolutionized advertising collectibles because it helps people find items quicker, and the increased supply holds down prices," Dotz said. Other recent trends Dotz noticed include:

• The emergence of new plush beanbags based on well-known advertising characters like Mr. Bubble and Speedy Alka-Seltzer.

• Booming interest in vinyl advertising collectibles from the 1960s and 1970s, compared to declining interest in advertising collectibles made of composition from the 1940s and 1950s.

• Fueled by the Internet, there's been an increased awareness of advertising characters from other countries like Toshiba Boy and Sony Boy.

• New commercials with retro characters like Charlie the Tuna, Mr. Whipple and Col. Sanders make younger collectors aware of vintage advertising characters they did not grow up with.

Kopleton said Funny Face mugs (remember Goofy Grape and Choo Choo Cherry?), Quisp, Cap'n Crunch, Tony the Tiger, Frankenberry, Boo Berry and Count Chocula are among the characters most in demand at her store.

"Monster collectors like them too," Kopleton said, referring to the General Mills cereal characters.

"Unusual Pillsbury Doughboy collectibles are also in demand," she added, referring to the Doughboy's family, including finger puppets of the Doughboy's grandparents.

According to Warren Dotz, pop culture historian and co-author of two books on advertising characters, other advertising toys and characters in demand with collectors include Reddy Kilowatt; the Hamm's Bear; vinyl Charlie the Tuna figures; bobbin' head dolls, especially Bob's Big Boy and Col. Sanders.; ESSO Oil banks; and the Raid Bug radio.

Demand is always strong for collectibles from classic companies like Texaco and Pillsbury, said Robert Reed, author of *Bears & Dolls In Advertising, Guide to Collectible Characters And Critters* (1998, Antique Trader Books/Krause Publications.)

Beanbag Market Cools Off

While the plush beanbag market is not "dead," it's not in robust health either, according to several dealers.

"It's surviving, but it's not booming," said Robert Audette, owner of five collectibles stores in North Carolina, Tennessee and Virginia. "Ty has dropped way off. It's [sales] a fraction of what it used to be. Overall, it's [the market] holding its own."

"Stagnant," was the word Steve Leiberman, manager of

The Top 10 Figural Model Kits
(in Mint in Box condition)

1. Godzilla's Go-Cart, Aurora, 1966 . . . .$6,520
2. Lost in Space, large scale kit with chariot, Aurora, 1966 1,485
3. Frankenstein, Gigantic 1:5 scale, Aurora, 1964 1,430
4. Munsters Living Room, diorama of Munsters characters in various positions, Aurora, 1964 1,430
5. King Kong's Thronester, Aurora, 1966 1,375
6. Lost in Space, small scale kit, Aurora, 1966 1,020
7. Lost in Space, The Robot, Aurora, 1968 880
8. Addams Family Haunted House, Aurora, 1964 880
9. Bride of Frankenstein, Aurora, 1965 .825
10. Penguin (Batman), Aurora, 1967 578

Archie's Collectibles in suburban Chicago, used to describe the plush beanbag market.

While Lieberman and Mick Tynski, manager of Diamond Card Exchange in Syracuse, N.Y., said Ty Beanie Babies remain the sales leaders at their stores, all dealers interviewed admitted Ty has lost its Midas touch on the market, especially in terms of the high prices Beanies brought at one time.

"Collectors are more aware," said Audette. "They realize if they're patient, they'll be able to find them [Beanies] eventually."

However, Dawn Schrock, manager of Paul & Judy's Coins & Cards in Arthur, Ill., said her store is still selling "as many [Ty Beanies], if not more [overall]."

"Prices are just more reasonable now," she said.

"A lot of people got into this thinking they were going to get rich," Audette stated. "They realize that's not the case. We try to tell them it's a hobby, not an investment."

In addition, dealers believed the plush beanbag market is oversaturated.

"Ty is keeping the market going, but others [lines] are also selling well," Tynski said.

And which would those be? Dealers cited:

• Booming orders for Liquid Blue's Grateful Dead Bears;

• Collecticritters. Schrock especially cited the VIP Senator set (a tribute to John Glenn) and the Graduation bear, a Dustin Hoffman tribute;

• Limited Treasures bears;

• Plant Plush bears;

• Titanic Trio bears.

Perhaps the biggest news in the

The Top 10 Coloring Books
(in Mint condition)

1. Courageous Cat and Minute Mouse, Artcraft $175
2. John Wayne Coloring Book, Saalfield, 1951 150
3. Hood's Sarsaparilla Painting Book, Hood, 1894 150
4. Gone with the Wind Paint Book, Merrill, 1940 150
5. Funny Company, Whitman, 1966 130
6. Touche Turtle, Whitman 125
7. Shirley Temple Crosses the Country, Saalfield, 1939 125
8. Draw & Paint Tom Mix, Whitman, 1935 125
9. Charlie Chaplin Up in the Air, M.A. Donahue & Co., 1914 125
10. Walt Disney's Mickey Mouse Paint Book, Whitman, 1937 110

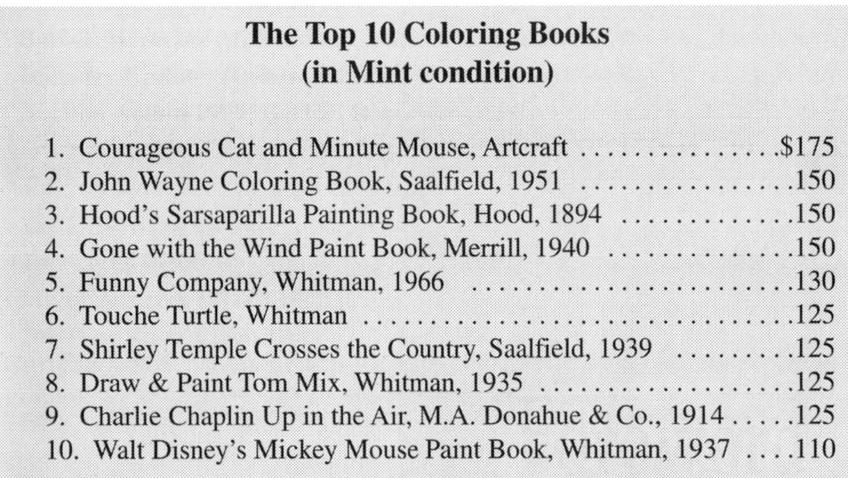

"Yellow Submarine" was huge in 1999 due to the reissue of the 1960s animated film. A Corgi die-cast Beatles' Yellow Submarine from the 1960s can bring $700 or more in pristine condition, but Corgi's repro Yellow Sub only runs $50.

beanbag hobby occurred late in the year when Ty posted one sentence on its web site that read "On December 31, 1999, 11:59 p.m. (CST) All beanies will be retired."

Rumors ran rampant that Ty was discontinuing production of Beanie Babies. Whether true or not, and toy experts believe the announcement simply meant that Ty is retiring all current Beanies, the statement did stir excitement in a stagnant hobby.

But if the plush market remains soft, dealers interviewed didn't appear worried. In fact, Audette said plush beanbags only represent 5 percent of his total sales.

"Winnie the Pooh, Rugrats, Scooby-Doo, we carry anything that's hot, that the kids are in to," he said.

If plush sales continue to stagnate, undoubtedly many dealers will turn to other toys to boost their bottom lines.

What's Old is New Again

While plush may have cooled off in 1999, perhaps the biggest surprise was the strong market for reproductions and new, never-before seen items of Beatles' *Yellow Submarine* toys, Hello Kitty, Aurora model kits, James Bond, *Lost in Space* model kits and lunch boxes, and others.

"The originals are becoming increasingly harder to find, and that's led to a boom in repros," said Mike Mitros, owner of the New Jersey-based M&J Variety. "Repros do fantastic [business] because they're so affordable."

Mitros pointed out that while an original King Seeley Thermos *Lost in Space* steel dome lunch box from 1967 can bring $1,000 in top condition, a repro *Lost in Space* dome by G Whiz retails for only $24.

Mitros said both original *Lost in Space* toys and *LIS* repros are in high demand at his store. "It seems the more valuable the original is, the more desirable the repro is," he said.

Playing Mantis/Polar Lights' reissues of vintage Aurora kits from the 1960s are good sellers, agreed Ohio dealer Jeff Perz.

"The original holds its value, but this way, people have one to build too," he said.

"A lot of companies have realized how popular the 1960s are and started doing repros," stated Mike Lombard, owner of a toy store in Nashville, Tenn.

Who's making the new toys?

"In some cases, they're new companies, but in other cases they're the same companies who did them originally," Lombard said.

For instance, Lombard stated that while Corgi's die-cast Beatles' *Yellow Submarine* from the 1960s can bring $700 to $800, Corgi's repro *Yellow Sub* only costs $50.

Do reproductions hurt the market for older toys? Dealers don't think so. In fact, Cheryl Traub, co-owner of

The Top 10 Battery-Operated Toys
(in Mint condition)

1. Mickey the Magician, Linemar, 1960s $2,500
2. Bubble Blowing Popeye, Linemar, 1950s 2,500
3. Gypsy Fortune Teller, Ichida, 1950s 2,200
4. Smoking Spaceman, Linemar, 1950s 1,600
5. Kooky-Spooky Whistling Tree, Marx, 1950s 1,600
6. Drumming Mickey Mouse, Linemar, 1950s 1,600
7. Nutty Nibs, Linemar, 1950s 1,400
8. Main Street, Linemar, 1950s 1,200
9. Tarzan, Marusan, 1960s 1,000
10. Super Susie, Linemar, 1950s 1,000

Not all collectors can afford (or even find) "Lost in Space" toys from the 1960s, that's why toys like this recent robot model kit by Playing Mantis/Polar Lights are becoming increasingly popular.

Frantic City Toys, said repros can actually lure new collectors into the hobby.

"People buy new stuff because of affordability, then they go after the older stuff," she said.

"If all someone has to spend is $50," Lombard said, "then yes, they'll buy the repro and not the original valued in the hundreds. On othe other hand, if someone is making $70,000 to $80,000 a year, they can afford the original. The price tag doesn't bother them a bit.

"Then," Lombard added, "there are the hard-core fans — and I've got some [James] Bond collectors — who buy both [the original and the repro]."

"There's always a market for the originals," Lombard noted.

Traub agreed. "Some people only go after vintage toys."

Ultimately, dealers said, the trick to a successful reproduction toy is to make it in numbers large enough that collectors can get their hands on them but not in numbers so limited that no one can find them.

"The key is to not flood the market, or they [the toys] end up on clearance racks," Lombard said.

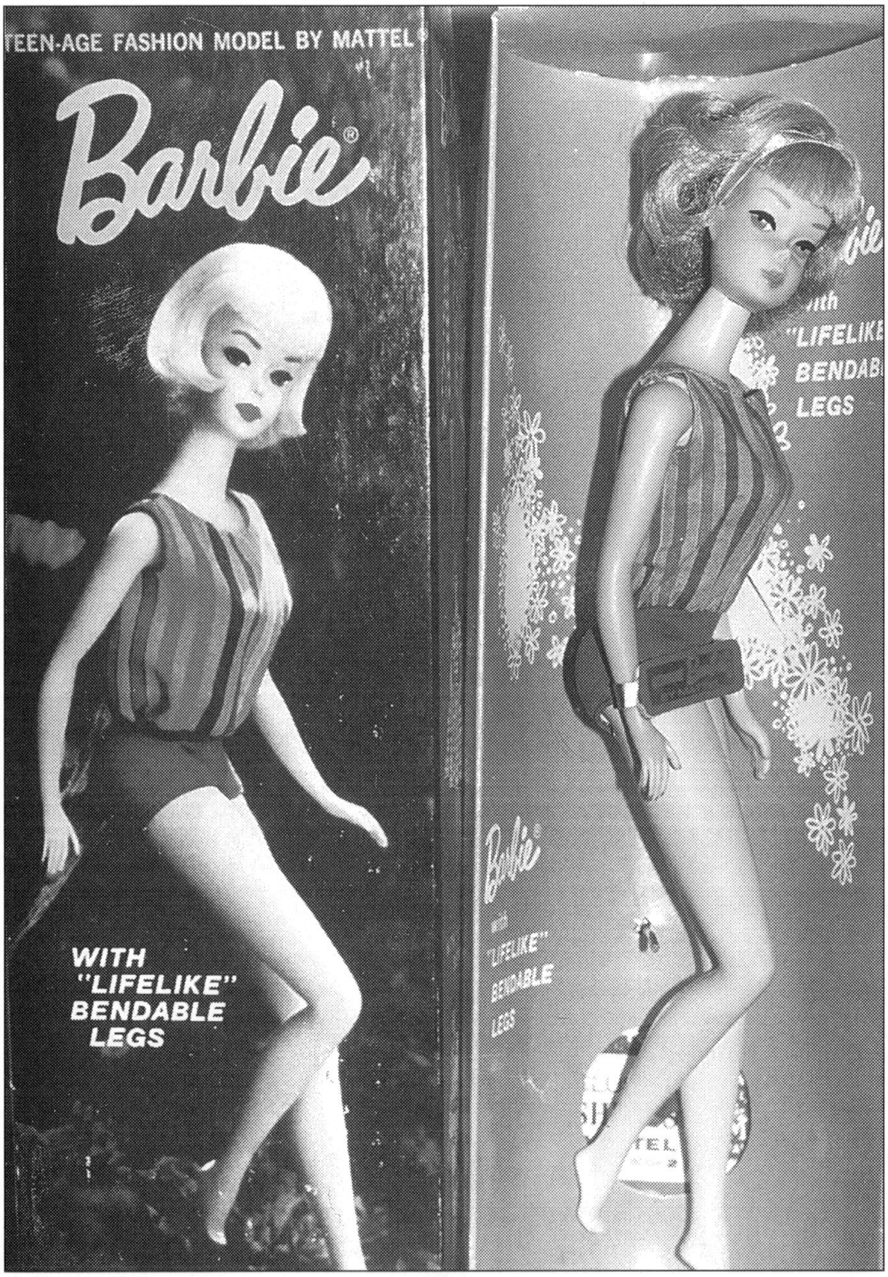

Die-Cast Vehicles

Where are the cars? That's what

The Top 10 Barbie Dolls
(in Mint in Box condition)

1. Ponytail Barbie #1, brunette, 1959 . . . .$9,000
2. Ponytail Barbie #1, blond, 1959 8,000
3. Ponytail Barbie #2, brunette, 1959 .7,000
4. Ponytail Barbie #2, blond, 1959 6,000
5. American Girl Side-Part Barbie, brunette, blond, titian, 1965 .4,000
6. Midge's Ensemble Gift Set, 1964 .3,200
7. Color Magic Barbie, midnight hair, 1966 3,200
8. Barbie's Round the Clock Gift Set, Bubblecut, 1964 3,000
9. Barbie Beautiful Blues Gift Set, 1967 3,000
10. Fashion Queen Barbie & Ken Trousseau Gift Set, 1964 2,800

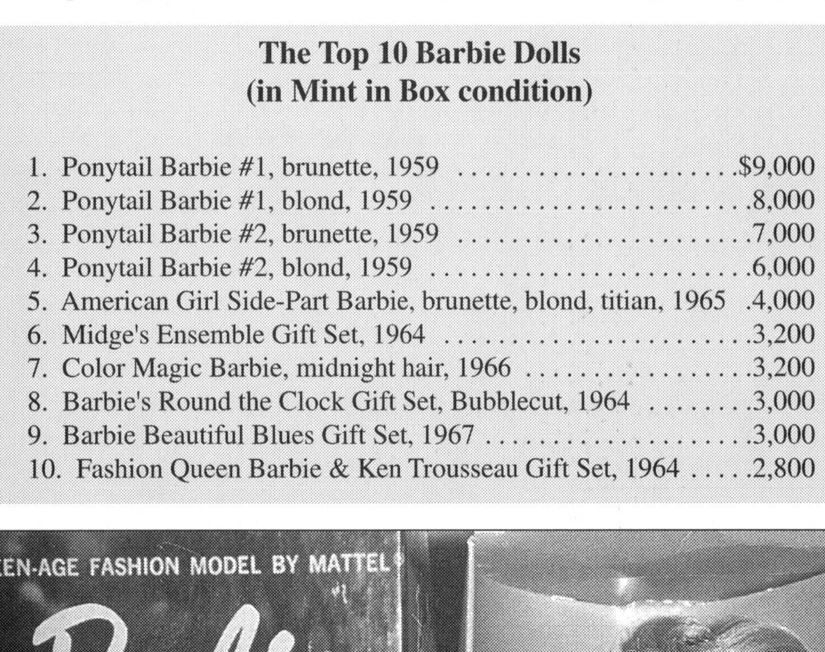

LEFT: American Girl Barbies from the 1960s can bring prices in the hundreds for loose dolls in Mint condition to thousands for Mint in Box specimens like this American Girl Side-Part. Photo courtesy of Marl Davidson. BELOW: While vintage Barbies from the 1960s and 1970s are always desirable, newer dolls like Soda Fountain Sweetheart from 1996 ($210) can also quickly bring good prices on the secondary market.

ABOVE: First Editions and other new Mattel Hot Wheels cars were increasingly difficult to find in 1999.

collectors of Mattel Hot Wheels cars lamented in 1999.

Jon Brecka, collector and Hot Wheels columnist for *Toy Shop* and *Toy Cars & Vehicles*, said that most long-awaited 1999 Hot Wheels cars should finally be arriving on store shelves by Christmas or early spring.

"Unfortunately," Brecka said, "that's the time that the new 2000 cars should be on the shelves, so it might be a while until collectors get more current with their collections."

Secondary market values for 1999 Hot Wheels Treasure Hunts remain excellent, Brecka said, with $15 to $20 for the unpopular models, $25 to $30 for more in demand

The Top 10 Mattel Classic Hot Wheels
(in Mint in Package condition)

1. Volkswagen Beach Bomb, surf boards in rear window, 1969 . $4,500
2. Custom Camaro, 1968, white enamel .2,000
3. Snake, 1973, white/yellow 1,500
4. Mongoose, 1973, red/blue 1,400
5. Mustang Stocker, 1975, white 1,200
6. Carabo, 1974, yellow 1,200
7. Custom Mustang, 1968 1,200
8. Mercedes C-111, 1973 1,200
9. Superfine Turbine, 1973 1,100
10. Ferrari 312P, 1973 1,100

The Top 10 Mattel Hot Wheels Numbered Packs
(in Mint in Package condition)

1. No. 51, '40s Woodie, 1987 . . . .$800
2. No. 49, Rolls-Royce, 1984 300
3. No. 242, '93 Camaro, 1993 200
4. No. 242, '93 Camaro, 1993 200
5. No. 75, Pontiac Banshee, 1990 200
6. No. 355, '67 Camaro, Treasure Hunts, 1995 200
7. No. 98, Nissan 300ZX, 1992 175
8. No. 94, Auburn 852, 1991 175
9. No. 88, T-Bird Stock, 1991 175
10. No. 2, '65 Mustang Convertible, 1987 165

The Top 10 Vehicle Toys
(in Mint condition)

1. Packard Straight 8, Hubley $15,000
2. Checker Cab, No. 175, Arcade 12,000
3. Elgin Street Sweeper, Hubley 11,500
4. World's Greatest Circus Truck, Keystone 10,000
5. Ingersoll-Rand Compressor, Hubley 10,000
6. Motorized Sidecar Motorcycle, Hubley 10,000
7. Ahrens-Fox Fire Engine, Hubley 8,000
8. Seven Man Fire Patrol, Hubley 7,500
9. Tractor Dredge (on Treads), Buddy L 7,500
10. White Bus, No. 319, Arcade 7,400

Harley-Davidson Barbie and Ken were striking 1999 debuts, now selling for $200 or more each.

models and $50 or more for the Mustang Mach I.

The Hot Wheels Cop Rods are selling for double or more their retail price on the secondary market, and the Hot Wheels Final Run cars are drawing more interest as they seem to have dried up on retail shelves, Brecka noted.

Die-cast NASCAR vehicles are in abundance, and Michigan dealer Jeff Clemence said any car with a Dale Earnhardt or Jeff Gordon theme will move. Interest was also noted at a summer show in the Midwest for 1960s Tonka trucks in pristine condition.

In addition, Brecka noted that, "Demand is strong for any of the [Playing Mantis] Johnny Lightning cars. In general, Johnny Lightning seems to be catching on with collectors."

Barbies in Demand

Ponytail Barbies from 1959 to 1962 are always in demand with collectors, but "Of course you have to have the pocketbook for it," stated Sandi Holder, owner of the Doll Attic in Union City, Calif.

Collectors are also clamoring for American Girl and Color Magic Barbies, noted Holder and Patricia Long, *Toy Shop* Barbie columnist.

Holder said American Girls dolls have been selling for $450 to $525 loose and in Mint condition and $995 or more for Mint in Box specimens.

Long said that collectors were not after different vintage Barbies than in years past.

"The same ones [dolls] are popular, but they're getting harder to find," Long said. "Any Barbie pre-1968 is in demand," she added.

Newer collector dolls are also good sellers, Holder and Long said.

Barbies and other 1999 dolls that were in demand at Holder's store included the Barbie Loves Frankie Sinatra set, $64; Mattel's Chatty Cathy reissue, $85; Millennium Bride, King Arthur and Queen Guinevere set, $80; and the Essence of Nature series Whispering Wind Barbie that sells for $64.

While the first two Harley-Davidson Barbies have quickly escalated in value on the secondary market, Holder said she has not received a lot of orders for them.

"Toys R Us is flooded with the third [Harley-Davidson Barbie], and I think people have given up on trying to find the older ones [the first and second Harley Barbies]," Holder said. "Personally, I don't think it's good for the hobby to have that new a doll going for that high a price."

BELOW: At $700 in Mint condition, Transogram's Jonny Quest Game from 1964 is one of the most desirable games on the secondary market.

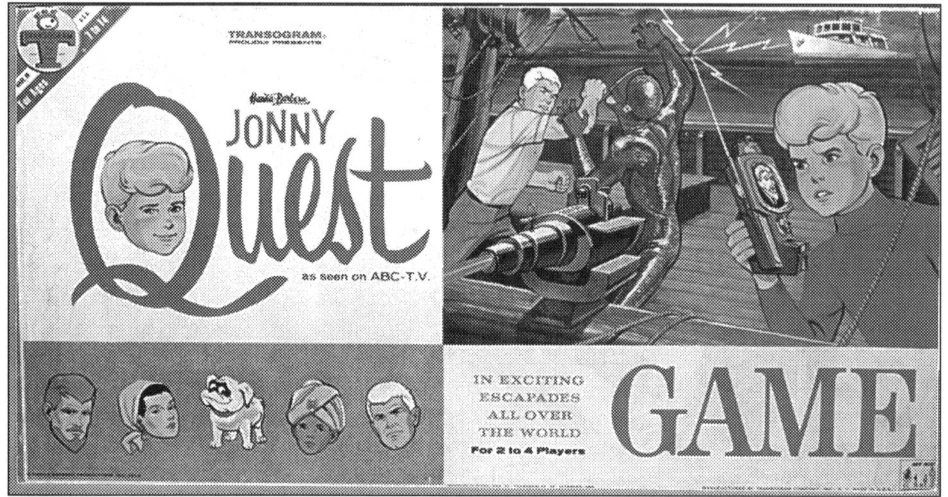

The Top 10 Prewar Games
(in Excellent condition)

1. Bulls and Bears, McLoughlin Bros., 1896 . . . .$13,000
2. New Parlor Game of Baseball, Sumner, 1896 10,000
3. Champion Baseball Game, Schultz, 1889 6,800
4. Little Fireman Game, McLoughlin Bros., 1897 6,000
5. Zimmer Baseball Game, McLoughlin Bros., 1885 6,000
6. Teddy's Ride from Oyster Bay to Albany, Jesse Crandall, 1899 5,500
7. Golf, Schoenhut, 1900 5,000
8. Egerton R. Williams Popular Indoor Baseball Game, Hatch, 1886 . . .5,000
9. Great Mails Baseball Game, Walter Mails Baseball Game, 1919 4,100
10. Darrow Monopoly, Charles Darrow, 1934 4,000

The Top 10 Postwar Games
(in Excellent condition)

1. Elvis Presley Game, Teen Age Games, 1957 . . . .$1,000
2. Red Barber's Big League Baseball Game, G & R Anthony, 1950s 900
3. Win A Card Trading Card Game, Milton Bradley, 1965 900
4. Munsters Drag Race Game, Hasbro, 1965 800
5. Munsters Masquerade Game, Hasbro, 1965 800
6. Creature From The Black Lagoon, Hasbro, 1963 750
7. Strike Three, Tone Products, 1948 725
8. Jonny Quest Game, Transogram, 1964 .700
9. Munsters Picnic Game, Hasbro, 1965 700
10. Challenge the Yankees, Hasbro, 1960s .700

Harley #1 from 1997 has brought $500, while Harley #2 from 1998 has sold for $150, according to Long.

But the most desirable Barbie of 1999 might be a 40th Anniversary Gala Barbie that was a gift from Mattel to attendees at a Barbie collectors convention in Pittsburgh, Pa. Not available at retail, the limited-edition (1,200) Barbie has brought prices ranging from $595 to $995, Holder said.

"Mattel has seen their weakness as far as overproducing [Barbies]," Holder said. "Make it [the production run] limited when it's supposed to be limited, and it works."

Other newer Barbies in demand, and their prices, according to Long include:

• Children's Collector Series Little Bo Peep from 1996, $150;

• Coca-Cola Fashion Series Soda Fountain Sweetheart (the first doll in the line), 1996, $210;

• Billions of Dreams, 1997, $350.

• Hollywood Legends *Wizard of Oz* Dorothy, 1994, cardboard lid, $245; plastic lid, $218;

• Runway Collection, In the Limelight, 1997, $175;

• Mattel Official Barbie Collectors Club grand premiere doll, 1997, $200.

Surprisingly, despite Mattel's decision to drop the popular Happy Holidays line, Holder said the dolls are not in demand at her store.

"The first one [from 1988] goes for $500 to $600 Mint in Box, but the rest [Happy Holidays Barbies] do not move as well," she stated.

And what about the Barbie market in general?

"Prices have stabilized," Holder said. "I don't see them going much higher. In terms of demand, I've gotten more re-orders than in the past, regardless whether it's a new or old doll."

The Top 10 Lunch Boxes
(in Near Mint condition)

1. 240 Robert, steel, Aladdin, 1978 ....$2,500
2. Toppie Elephant, steel, American Thermos, 1957 1,600
3. Home Town Airport Dome, steel, King Seeley Thermos, 1960 ...1,000
4. Underdog, steel, Okay Industries, 1974 900
5. Knight in Armor, steel, Universal, 1959 825
6. Ballerina, vinyl, Universal, 1960s 800
7. Superman, steel, Universal, 1954 800
8. Dudley Do-Right, steel, Universal, 1962 800
9. Bullwinkle & Rocky, steel, Universal, 1962 800
10. Little Friends, vinyl, Aladdin, 1982 760

Fun and Games

Mystery Date and Dark Tower top two dealers' lists of most-requested games.

Mystery Date ($100 to $150 in Excellent to Mint condition), Milton Bradley's game of social significance, is obviously popular among women since it was designed for girls, but it also has a following in New York's gay community.

Dark Tower, a Milton Bradley game from 1981, could be the only electronic game that's a hot item. Dark Tower brings prices ranging from $150 to as much as $200.

Other top-selling games and their prices, according to dealers Lyle Rhodebeck and Jeff Lowe include:

• Pollyanna, Parker Brothers, 1952, $40 to $60;

• Nancy Drew, Parker Brothers, 1957 or 1959 versions, $70 to $100;

• Park and Shop, Milton Bradley, 1953, $50 to $75;

• Pit, Parker Brothers, especially 1973 version that includes an orange bell, $15 to $25;

• King Oil, Milton Bradley, 1974, $25 to $50;

• Voice of the Mummy, Milton Bradley, 1971, $75 to $125;

• Gamemaster Series games, Milton Bradley, 1980s, especially: Broadsides & Boarding Parties, $100 to $150; Conquest of the Empire, $100 to $150; Shogun, $60 to $100,

• Green Ghost, Transogram, 1965, $85 to $120;

• Monopoly, Parker Brothers: Darrow games, $1,100; rare prewar games, $75 to $100; rare postwar versions, $50 to $75; foreign sets, $60 to $90;

• King of the Hill, Schaper, 1960s, $50 to $75;

• True Colors, Milton Bradley, 1990, $35 to $55;

• Talisman, Games Workshop (game itself — supplements add to value), $75 to $150;

• Which Witch?, Milton Bradley, 1970, $45 to $75.

The Top 10 A.C. Gilbert Erector Sets
(in Excellent condition)

1. Set #10, Complete Erector in all its Glory, 1929-31, oak chest $7,875
2. Set #10, Complete Deluxe Set, 1928, nine-drawer oak chest 7,875
3. Set #10, Erector Deluxe in all its Glory, 1927, eight-drawer oak chest 7,875
4. Set #10, 1920-26, wood box 7,875
5. Set #9, Mechanical Wonders Set with 110-Volt Motor, 1929-32, wood box .4,610
6. Set #8-1/2, 1931-32, wood box 3,150
7. Set #7-1/2, Motorized Erector, 1914, wood box 1,575
8. Set #12-1/2, 1956-57, metal box 1,365
9. Set #12-1/2, 1948-50, metal box 1,365
10. Set #10093, 1959, metal box 1,265

Happy Anniversary!
Queen Barbie and King G.I. Joe Celebrated in 1999

The anticipation for the new millennium to arrive was great in 1999. But the toy world was celebrating all throughout 1999.

The toy industry's king and queen — G.I. Joe and Barbie — both celebrated birthdays with much fanfare. But they weren't the only toy icons being honored.

The following is a look at some of the toy greats that hit milestones in 1999.

90 YEARS
Kewpies

When Rose O'Neill's Kewpies appeared in their first story called *The Kewpies and the Airplane* in 1909, O'Neill probably had no idea her chubby little cherubs would become a sensational doll hit.

Soon after, more stories followed and children pleaded for a Kewpie they could actually hold. O'Neill herself sculpted the first Kewpie doll and a German manufacturer produced them. The craze was so big that the company had to have 30 factories working on just these dolls.

Now, Kewpies can be found in many forms, ranging anywhere from $100 to $2,000 for vintage examples depending on their condition, look and rarity.

80 YEARS
Felix the Cat

When Otto Messmer was asked by his boss Pat Sullivan to design a cartoon character for *Paramount Screen Magazine*, he started to dabble with a quick-drawn black cat.

Using a lot of picture gags, Messmer's new character, Felix, was constantly outwitted by a little mouse. Though some criticized Felix as looking like a dog with angular features, Felix grew in popularity and became the first cartoon character to hit the big screen.

Because of his black and white coloring and his simple angles, he was perfect for quick, easy animation. The stories were generally good and the gags hilarious, but the development of a personality in Felix was what led to his ultimate success.

With a wink or a twist of his tail, Felix had the crowds rolling in their seats, making him the greatest cartoon star in the silent era. With his bag of tricks and his versatile tail, Felix could squeeze himself out of the toughest situations.

Cartoons without voices will always have something to say, especially if Felix has any part.

70 YEARS
Warner Brothers

The year was 1929, and Disney

That crazy Felix the Cat turned 80 in 1999.

LEFT: German bisque Kewpie dolls.

RIGHT: Bugs Bunny and Elmer Fudd are two popular Warner Bros. characters.

had just lost two great animators, Hugh Harman and Rudolph Ising, to the Warner brothers who were about to make cartoon history.

Jack and Harry Warner started adding animation to their music catalogues to add interest. Then in 1930, the first Looney Tunes cartoon was born. Titled *Sinkin' in the Bathtub*, it starred Bosko the Talk-Ink Kid. From then on, audiences identified Warner Brothers with sly wit, split-second timing and a playfulness that was popular with all ages.

The first fully-developed Looney Tunes star was Porky Pig, who appeared in *I Haven't Got a Hat* in 1935. Other boisterous characters to follow were Daffy Duck in 1937, Bugs Bunny in 1940, Tweety Bird in 1942 and Sylvester in 1945.

As popularity goes, Looney Tunes finally had the chance to make their feature film debut in the late 1990s in *Space Jam* starring Michael Jordan. Looney Tunes still appear on Saturday morning cartoons, enchanting a new generation.

55 YEARS

Monopoly

Submitted to Parker Brothers by Charles B. Darrow in 1934, Monopoly is the best-selling and most well-known game in the world today.

Initially turned down unanimously by company executives, Darrow set out on his own and produced 5,000 copies of his game and sold them to Wannamaker's store in Philadelphia.

When Parker Brothers saw the success of the game, they reconsidered and bought the rights.

Now the game is published in 40 countries translated into foreign currency and real estate and is printed in 25 languages including Icelandic and Croatian. Other editions include edible version made out of chocolate, a gold and silver edition that sold for $25,000, a Braille edition and a life-size reproduction.

ABOVE: Parker Brothers updated its famous Clue game for the game's 50th anniversary. It added a new weapon — a bottle of poison. BELOW RIGHT: The infectious charm of Disney's Donald Duck is evident in many toys and collectibles.

50 YEARS

Clue

The classic "whodunit" myster endures in a game where you and your closest playmates had a weapon of choice and a killer among friends.

The Parker Brothers game was imported from England as Cluedo, the Sherlock Holmes Game in 1948 and released to the public in 1949 as Clue. The first versions included a separate parts box, and the rope weapon was real rope (not plastic). Early versions are sought by collectors; later versions are too common to have much value.

Until now, the game remained the same. But to celebrate Clue's anniversary, Parker Brothers has released a new weapon, a bottle of poison — just a subtle twist to tell the world that a little change is good, even for the classics.

45 YEARS

Donald Duck

The most dramatic of Disney's comic characters, Donald Duck, was the last to get his big shot in toys and on the silver screen.

Of all the characters that appeared in the cartoons along with Mickey Mouse, Donald was the ultimate supporting actor. This impatient tantrum-throwing duck personified wackiness.

Magic 8-Ball

Fortune telling and future guessing is a trade ancient to the world and only gypsies and witches with crystal balls could tell you the truth.

But the Alabe Crafts Company in Cincinnati decided to let us in on all the fun. In 1946, they created a novelty version of the crystal ball the size of a grapefruit, and, when flipped upside down, revealed the answers to life's most difficult questions.

Forget the fortune cookie and the William Fuld's Mystifying Oracle, the Ouija board, the Magic 8-ball revealed everything needed to know. And what's even more amazing is that the 20 possible answers, 10 being positive, five negative and five neutral, statisticians say the ball has a high degree of accuracy. Whoa.

40 YEARS

Barbie

When Mattel co-founder Ruth Handler saw her daughter Barbara playing with paper dolls, she realized that playing make-believe was a necessity in growing up.

After finding the market void of young adult fashion dolls, Handler decided to fill the gap with the three-dimensional fashion doll every girl would love. However, her all-male staff wasn't quite so excited.

After several designs, Barbie was shown at Toy Fair in 1959 and toy buyers were shocked at the doll's ample bosom. Moving ahead, undaunted, Mattel used innovative television ads to reach their target audience instantly and the sensational Barbie was born.

Barbie went through a new face sculpting in 1967, gained a boyfriend in 1961 and a best friend, Midge, in 1963. She has sports cars, mansions, and a wardrobe any star would die for. In the last few years, Barbie's taken on diverse occupations and has

Fred Gwynne, Yvonne DeCarlo and Al Lewis starred in TV's "The Munsters."

become available in more high-tech forms.

Etch-a-Sketch

Though created by garage mechanic Arthur Granjean in 1958, the Etch-A-Sketch was taken to a toy fair in Nuremberg, Germany, in 1959 where it was viewed by the Ohio Art Company.

Though they initially rejected the toy, Ohio Art invested $25,000 in the license (five times more than they had paid for a license before) and the L'Ecran Magique was on its way.

With redeveloping and reworking, the ultimate Etch-A-Sketch arrived.

The toy has remained virtually unchanged for 40 years.

35 YEARS

G.I. Joe

Ever since his introduction in 1964, G.I. Joe has been everyone's top man. He's been Hasbro's largest on-going series of modern action figures, and his collectibility is infinite.

G.I. Joe was created in 1964 as a 12-inch moveable "doll" for boys, who could be dressed in a variety of uniforms with an array of accessories. A stroke of marketing genius was to call G.I. Joe an "action figure," the first of its kind to carry that moniker.

Throughout 35 years, G.I. Joe has undergone changes in design, look, size and occupation. It remains the king of collectible toys, alongside his 40-year-old counterpoint queen, Barbie.

The Munsters

When Herman Munster walked onto the TV screen, the only screams heard from the audience were fits of laughter.

All heart, Herman's family enchanted the audience with their slapstick comedy and a strangely common way of life. They lived at 1313 Mockingbird Lane with their pet dragon Spot, Igor the family bat, and the ever-present, ever-annoying cuckoo clock named Raven.

Though their cancellation in 1966 removed them from their initial big break, *The Munsters* still runs in syndication, and the characters are popular toys. Some of the more collectible toys include dolls, lunch boxes and puppets. The enthusiasm for these spooky toys shows the world this strange movie family is here to stay.

The Addams Family

In 1964, cartoonist Charles Addams' popular *The New Yorker* cartoon family of oddballs hit the TV screen with stars like John Astin, Carolyn Jones and child star

Those unmistakable eyes! Mattel's Barbie is still queen of collectible toys even after 40 years.

Hasbro's G.I. Joe has undergone many changes in 35 years, but his soul of bravery and good has remained.

Jackie Coogan.

The show combined morbid humor with strange props and guests including Cleopatra the man-eating plant, Wednesday's headless doll, and cousin ITT. Today, Addams Family puzzles, board games and Thing banks still show up on the secondary market. They may have been creepy, kooky, and just a little spooky, but people love them anyway. Heck, maybe that's why they love 'em.

20 YEARS
Happy Meal Toys

Fast food toys seem like they've been around forever, but McDonald's Happy Meal toys are only a generation old.

The first national Happy Meal promotion was released in 1979 with the Circus Wagon Happy Meal.

The first big promotion was for *Star Trek* in 1979, which sold five different boxes and included toys like navigation wrist bracelets, video communicators, secret compartment rings, crew badges and iron-on transfers of the crew.

Over the short 20 years, McDonald's has featured licensed toys like Walt Disney, Barbie, Play-Doh, Muppet Babies, Hot Wheels and Beanie Babies.

BELOW: How many McDonald's Happy Meals have you eaten just to get the toys?

10 YEARS
The Simpsons

If you've ever wondered how much TV has changed over the years, *The Simpsons* is an extreme for the present. Being a cartoon, the show's sarcastic humor was initially overlooked by TV viewers.

With characters like dimwitted Homer and the world's greatest underachiever, Bart, it was soon to

Ty's Beanie Babies, slated to be retired at the end of 1999, have taken the collecting world by storm for the last five years.

be a hit, showing the real world that TV land isn't always full of wonderfully-behaved children and parents that have the perfect answer for everything.

5 YEARS
Beanie Babies

With the Beanie Baby craze still in full swing, how did it all begin?

In early 1994, Ty released the original nine beanies which included Spot the dog, Chocolate the moose, Patti the Platypus, Cubbie the bear, Flash the dulphin, Legs the frog, Pinchers the lobster, Splash the whale, and Squealer the pig.

Retired in early 1997, they became rabidly sought collectibles. Then with the first McDonald's Teenie Beanie Baby promotion, thousands of new collectors joined the race.

Early Beanies don't come cheap. With Cubbie realizing

$3,700 and the others not far behind, some collectors hold a fortune on their shelves and will never give it up.

The company's late 1999 announcement that it would retire all Beanie Babies fueled speculation that the successful line would end. But a new year may bring with it new promise and new products from the Illinois company.

1 YEAR
Toy Cars & Vehicles

In 1998, 10 years after the debut of *Toy Shop*, Krause Publications introduced a monthly magazine devoted specifically to toys and models on wheels. *Toy Cars & Vehicles* stemmed from the acquisition of *Model Car Journal*, a publication targeted at model kit builders.

Toy Cars & Vehicles not only contains kit building information, but has broadened its scope to include everything from scale models to toys. Other areas such as promotional vehicles, Hot Wheels, farm toys and precision models are also covered.

In late 1999, the magazine underwent a format change. The tabloid newspaper size publication was revamped as a glossy, colorful newsstand magazine.

The Science of Grading Toys

Use Good Judgment, Research Before You Buy

By Sharon Korbeck

Think that action figure you're trying to sell is *really* in Mint condition?

Maybe to you it is, but far too often, people advertise Mint condition toys that are, actually, far from that condition.

Maybe it's ignorance or wishful thinking. But whatever the reason, dealers past and present have continued to overestimate the condition of their toys. And many unassuming, or unknowledgeable, collectors have fallen victim.

Offering lesser condition toys for top prices is far too prevalent in the hobby — and it will continue unless more people become educated about how to grade toys reasonably.

Grading scales vary from dealer to dealer, publication to publication and collector to collector. Even geography plays a role.

The reasons for buying toys may also determine what a collector is willing to pay. Some people seek toys in the best possible condition for investment purposes; others may seek the same toy in any condition for nostalgic reasons.

While grading is an imperfect science, here are some tips to keep in mind.

1. Packaging. Most toys originally packaged on cards or in boxes command higher prices in their new, pristine condition even though they may be more beautiful outside the package. Questions to ask yourself about packaging include: Does the box exhibit shelf wear? Are the edges worn or lightened in color? Does a blister card have a crease or scratches? Is the plastic bubble perfect?

2. Material. What is the toy made of and how sturdy is that material? For example, paper items (like boxes, paper dolls and coloring books) will likely exhibit some wear over time. Some wear on these items may be acceptable to collectors; major wear, however, may not. Cast-iron toys, which should have held up better over time, should be judged differently than toys made of less-sturdy construction.

3. Age of Item. When was the toy originally made? Late 1800s? 1950s? 1990s? A collector buying a toy from the early 1900s may be willing to accept a lesser-condition item since so few examples may still exist (and the toy has had to survive over 90 years). But toys from the past 20 years often must be in much better condition to entice buyers, unless the toy is ultra-rare or desirable.

4. Appearance and Function. These two factors are often vital to the collector, and they go hand in hand. For example, a vintage Fisher-Price pull toy may look great, but does it work as it was originally intended?

Offering lesser condition toys for top prices is far too prevalent in the hobby.

Some collectors, however, may not care whether or not a toy is operational as long as it looks good for display purposes.

Toy Shop has adopted the following grading descriptions. Remember, however, no single grading system will apply to all toys. Some descriptions may not apply to certain toys depending on how they are categorized, when they were produced, how they were originally packaged and how they are collected today.

MIB / MIP (Mint in Box, Mint in Package): Just like new in original package. The box may have been opened, but inside packages remain unopened. New toys in factory-sealed boxes may command higher prices. A comparable rating used in other guides may be "C-10."

MNB / MNP (Mint no Box, Mint no Package): This is also known as "loose" condition. A toy in Mint condition but not in its original package.

NM (Near Mint): A toy that looks new in overall appearance, but exhibits very minor wear and does not have the original box. An exception would be a toy that comes in kit form. A kit in Near Mint condition would be expected to have the original box, but the box may display some wear.

EX (Excellent): A toy that is complete and has been played with. Signs of minor wear may be evident, but the toy is very clean and well cared for.

GD (Good): A toy that obviously has been played with and shows general wear overall. Paint chipping is readily apparent. In metal toys, some minor rust may be evident. In sets, some minor pieces may be missing.

Compare our grading system with others you may encounter. The basic tenets of condition and appearance apply, although perhaps at different levels. For example, the O'Brien's *Collecting Toys* books use a C6, C8, C10 grading system, which compares fairly closely to Good, Excellent and Mint conditions.

Decide what type of collector you want to be — the level of money you are willing to spend, the amount of return (if any) you hope to reap from your investments and the amount of time you will devote to your hobby.

So, learn the jargon, develop a sharp eye for subtleties, compare grading scales and decide what a toy is worth to you. You can turn the subjective field of toy collecting into a rewarding objective for yourself.

Barbie Meets the Millennium

Can't Find Your Dream Doll? Make Her at www.barbie.com

By Sharon Korbeck

What technological breakthrough has literally changed the face of a 20th-century icon?

Cloning? Gender selection? Laser vision correction?

Actually, it's nothing quite as complicated.

Mattel's My Design, an online program located at *www.barbie.com*, lets kids, collectors and aspiring designers personalize a doll of their dreams — their very own "friend of Barbie."

Barbie did, after all, turn 40 this year (time for a facelift, maybe?). It was an appropriate time for Mattel to leap headfirst into Internet technology, preparing Barbie for the next millennium and, in turn, meeting the needs of Internet-savvy buyers.

"It was very unique for us to use the Internet in that way," Lisa McKendall, Mattel's director of marketing and public relations, said of My Design, which debuted in late 1998.

"One of the great things about the Internet is that it is always changing," McKendall added. That chameleon-like quality allows buyers and designers to change their doll's hairstyles, fashions and personalities in several clicks of a mouse. But how does it work?

Buyers can customize the doll on the screen, print and save their design, then, if desired, order the doll for $40.

"There aren't limitless possibilities," she said, so processing the orders isn't a production nightmare for Mattel. Here's how it works.

Step One: Name game. This is where the real value of the My Design doll lies. Kids thrill to opening a Barbie pink box bearing their name. It's just plain cool. Pranksters' alert —

ABOVE: Abby Gerbers is one of many little girls to own a My Design doll fashioned after her image. BELOW: The packaging of the My Design doll features a personalized profile of the doll, including name, birthday and hobbies.

don't try to name a doll after a porn queen; the program contains a "naughty word filter."

Step Two: Saving face. Buyers can choose from four skin tones, three eye colors, four hairstyles and six hair colors (sorry, Dennis Rodman, no neon green allowed). All options are realistic and stylish, but none allow much creativity.

After each attribute is selected, an image of the doll appears on the screen, and changes can be made at any time.

Step Three: Move over, Calvin Klein. Selecting the doll's facial attributes is pretty basic, but the fun part is playing fashion designer and choosing the doll's apparel.

Choices change frequently, McKendall said, as fashions sell out. No Mackie designs here (it is, after all, a fairly inexpensive

doll), but the My Design doll can quickly move from the MTV generation (denim jacket, funky dress and work boots) to the ballroom crowd (elegant purple evening gown) to the Nancy Sinatra look (how about a funky red vinyl duster and black go-go boots?).

Step Four: Getting to know you. What would a personalized doll be without a personality? A brief paragraph, printed on the doll's box, will describe the doll's customized persona. Again, choices are limited, but they include everything from astronomy and psychology to movies, boys and surfing the Web!

Step Five: Bring 'er home. Barring any computer glitches — and there have been some; one early glitch lost hundreds of orders — the ordering process runs smoothly. A credit card secures the order; dolls have routinely shipped in two to three weeks.

The success of Mattel's site has so far been measured only by buyers' satisfaction. McKendall said Mattel never discloses production numbers on any Barbie line, and she failed to provide figures on how many hits *www.barbie.com* has received. She did mention, however, that overall site traffic to the barbie.com site has

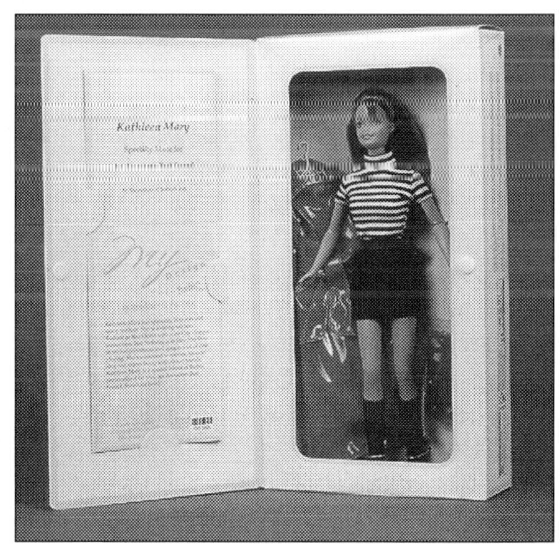

increased by 400 percent since the addition of the My Design program in November, 1998.

While many buyers have been pleased with the quality of the dolls, some feel $40 is too high for a basic play doll with little customization capabilities and a rather plain package. Forty dollars is a starting price for Mattel's collector edition dolls; most My Design dolls, however, are purchased for children to play with.

Children and beginning Barbie fans are the likely target for My Designs. It's unlikely serious collectors will embrace My Design dolls, especially for investment purposes. Because My Design dolls are basically the same doll in the same package (with minor, insignificant differences), there is the potential for millions to be produced. And those are poor odds that the dolls will increase in value.

As gifts, however, the product is a resounding success. And the design process has become smoother and quicker with fewer computer snags and easier click-throughs.

Isn't technology great? Just think, with just a few clicks of your mouse, your dream girl can be delivered directly to your door in just two weeks.

Of course, she'll only be 12 inches tall . . .

Surfing the World Wide Web With Barbie

If you've begun to notice a strange pink glow around your computer, you may be visiting too many Barbie sites. That's easy to do — there are many.

Some are quite well done and offer valuable information and links. Others are often littered with unfounded gossip and rumors (it can be fun to dish between collectors, as long as site visitors realize the information exchanged is often not verified).

For the most authoritative information about Barbie, Mattel's site, *www.barbie.com*, is the only official source to visit. In addition to being the home of the My Design site, the site targets its content at parents and collectors as well as children. It is the definitive source for accurate information about Mattel's newest lines, but you won't find secondary market information here.

One of the best sites we visited was *www.flash.net/~dsquard7*. The site's strength is in its dozens of valuable links. Want to order a Barbie book or video? This site links you directly to amazon.com. What's new in exclusives? A quick link to FAO Schwarz will picture that store's high-end exclusive Barbies. And, of course, a link to eBay puts buyers in direct link with the thousands of Barbies for sale daily on the auction site.

Another superior site is brought to viewers from the folks at about.com — who purport to have experts in dozens of fields from collecting to gardening. Sarah Locker is the expert "hosting" the Barbie collecting site, located at barbiedolls.miningco.com. The cleanly-organized site has all the basics for beginners and more in-depth info (and chat rooms) for fans.

Got a question? Locker has covered the FAQs swiftly. Don't know what NRFB means (that's Barbie talk for "Never Removed from Box")? Locker dispenses the jargon newbie collectors need to sound "in the know."

Want a fresh new look for Barbie? The All Dolled Up site, *www.toad.net/~anardone/*, offers "one-of-a-kind" designs. Not a graphically-stunning site, it does offer Barbie fans a source for rerooting doll hair and facial repaints.

For fans across the Northern border, check out the Barbie Goes to Canada site at *www.odyssee.net/~tesla/home.html*. A timeline of Barbie milestones is included. The info is not new to the veteran collector, but it is a quick-and-easy reference for new enthusiasts. Canadian fans of Barbie will also find references to clubs, magazines and shows based in their country.

One of the more active chat rooms for Barbie fans exists at The Doll Page, *www.dollpage.com*. The Pink Chat room is an active and opinionated arena; adult content, however, may make the site often inappropriate for youth.

Consider yourself an eavesdropper? The Barbie Newbie Page tends to be gossip central with its "Babs Talk Babbler." At *www.geocities.com/FashionAvenue/4060/* you can get in on chats with worldwide collectors and Barbie fans. Be aware, however, that the gossip on this site is often unfounded, unverified rumor.

Your best bet to find more hot Barbie links? You could go the general search engine route, looking under "Barbie" or "Barbie Dolls," but some of the best links we found are at *www.flash.net/~dsquard7*.

The Four Most Controversial Barbies

From bust size to sexual orientation, Mattel's Barbie has faced and, for the most part, fended off many controversies.

As times changed, so did America's icon. So it's only fitting that her political correctness be scrutinized by everyone.

Here's a quick look at the four most talked-about Barbies.

1. Growing Up Skipper, 1977. Barbie's bust size has always been questioned. But with this version of Barbie's little sister, that problem seemed, well, small. When Skipper's shoulders were twisted, her waist shrunk and her bustline grew. Toy manufacturers have learned by now not to mess with a doll's anatomy. **Value today: $35**

2. Earring Magic Ken, 1993. Dressed in flashy purple attire and adorned with an earring, Ken's sexuality was open to interpretation. Right-wing groups had a field day with this one. C'mon guys, it's just a toy. **Value today: $25.**

3. Teen Talk Barbie, 1992. It's often best to think before speaking. Mattel violated this rule when it made its trendy teen talker say, "Math class is tough." Try telling that to women's groups who argued the phrase evoked a negative image. While the phrase subtracted from the doll's image then, it has amounted to major popularity among collectors. **Value today: $400 for the offending variation; a mere $15 for others.**

4. Teacher Barbie, 1985. A doll without underwear? That's what rankled the masses when this short-skirted doll debuted in the mid-1980s. The lack of underclothing created much dissent; Mattel finally remedied the situation with paint. **Value today: $15.**

Mattel's New Mantra

Looming large over New York's Avenue of the Americas is a black and white billboard depicting the sunkissed face of a young girl. Stark pink lettering heralds a simple message — "Be anything."

Subtle. Understated. Eye-catching. Mattel's new ad campaign encompasses everything its trademark doll stands for. That's why Mattel's new mantra — "be anything" — hits its mark powerfully.

Television and print ads began running early this year depicting young girls of many cultures.

As Barbie celebrates four decades of aspirations, glamour, fantasy and dreams, Mattel has taken a new approach to marketing the doll to a new generation of girls.

"Overall, the Barbie collection encourages girls to participate in the world they are discovering . . . Barbie inspires girls to be anything," according to Mattel press information.

Barbie, herself, has been just about everything throughout her timeless 40 years. Among her more memorable careers are astronaut, paleontologist, Olympic athlete and doctor.

In 1999, Barbie became a Working Woman (licensed by the magazine of the same name), Major League Baseball player and member of the Women's World Cup Soccer team.

What will Barbie be in 2000? Elizabeth Dole as Commander in Chief? Ken as First Man?

Near Monopoly?

Hasbro Strengthens Force in Games Market

By Mike Jacquart

Could Hasbro, maker of popular games like Monopoly, be gaining a near monopoly of its own in the game industry?

Hasbro, which already owns Milton Bradley and Parker Brothers, reportedly paid $325 million for the Seattle-based Wizards of the Coast, makers of the Pokémon trading card game as well as the popular Magic: The Gathering and Dungeons & Dragons games.

Some dealers were concerned that Hasbro will make retail stores the main channel of distribution for both Pokémon and Magic. "That's the big fear," said Scott Wool, owner of the Omni Cards & Comics chain in Connecticut. "Once you make something readily available, it isn't collectible anymore. Hasbro doesn't have a good history of working with the hobby."

But Wayne Charness, Hasbro's senior vice president, told the Associated Press that his company does not intend to make his newly-acquired gaming properties mass-

Krause Publications Buys Competitor; Changes Format of One Magazine, Launches Another

Krause Publications, publisher of *Toy Shop*, announced its largest acquisition to date in 1999 — the purchase of Landmark Specialty Publications headquartered in Norfolk, Va. Key publications included *Antique Trader Weekly, Toy Trader, Tuff Stuff, Big Reel* and *Discoveries.*

Toy Trader was later merged with *Toy Shop* magazine.

Krause President Clifford Mishler said the move will "bring even more expertise under our roof and further solidify our position as the world's largest hobby publisher. It is a natural fit for these two companies to come together."

In addition to the blockbuster acquisition of one of its largest competitors, Krause Publications also changed the look of one toy magazine and launched a new magazine.

Beginning with its November/December 1999 issue, *Toy Cars & Vehicles* switched from a newspaper stock format to a colorful, glossy tabloid. "Our readers and advertisers have asked for a magazine style with more color and we certainly want to meet our customers' needs with the best product possible," said Publisher Mark Williams.

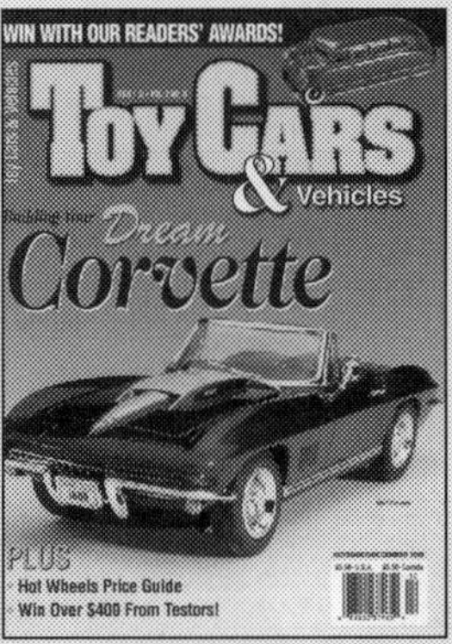

ABOVE: "Toy Cars & Vehicles" first glossy cover. RIGHT: The toy magazine's old look.

Associate Editor Merry Dudley was also excited about the change. "We have photographs of beautiful high-end models costing hundreds of dollars that simply were not done justice by the black-and-white pictures. *Toy Cars & Vehicles* has some of the best collecting editorial content available on the subject. The new design provides visuals that live up to the quality of the editorial material."

Toy Cars & Vehicles celebrated its one-year anniversary in March 1999. The magazine caters to collectors of model kits, die-casts, motor sports, farm toys, promotional models and others.

Krause Publications also began publishing *eBay Magazine* in September. The monthly lifestyle publication is geared to the millions of Internet-savvy collecting consumers who are buying items on the Internet and have made going online part of their daily lives.

The magazine includes tips for navigating the Internet, feature stories on celebrity collectors and advice for finding elusive collectibles.

market products. Instead, he said the acquisition was designed to strengthen its game lineup.

"It expanded our opportunities in games, which is a cornerstone of our growth industry," Charness said.

Wizards President Peter Adkison agreed.

"The success of this company [Wizards]," Adkison said, "relies on the hobby channel of distribution. Hasbro felt they didn't have the right products or connections [to make money in the hobby game market]; now they do."

What Wizards gained is greater financial stability in a market known for severe ups and downs.

The amount is by far the most ever paid for an adventure game company. In 1998, Hasbro bought Avalon Hill for $7 million. The sale price translates to about $900 per share in privately-held Wizards stock.

Several major die-cast acquisitions were also announced in 1999.

Zindart Limited purchased Corgi Classics Limited. Zindart, founded in 1978 and boasting over $100 million in revenues, produces and markets high-quality die-cast and injection-molded collectibles. The purchase price for Corgi, another manufacturer of collectible scale vehicles, was approximately $46 million.

Racing Champions, makers of die-cast NASCAR collectibles, bought the Iowa-based Ertl Co., a market leader in agricultural and custom imprint die-cast collectibles. Terms of the deal were not disclosed, but Ertl's corporate revenues for the 1998 fiscal year totaled $175 million.

Bob Dods, Racing Champions chairman and CEO said the purchase of Ertl would bring "significant opportunities to expand the combined companies' strong presence in all categories of die-cast collectibles including NASCAR, custom and classic and agricultural."

In other acquisitions, JAKKS Pacific, named by *Fortune* magazine as the ninth fastest-growing company in 1999, announced two major purchases.

The firm, known for its wrestling action figures, purchased the privately-held Berk Corp., the leading producer of educational toy foam puzzles, mats and blocks.

The Berk line includes licensed characters such as Mickey Mouse, Winnie the Pooh, Teletubbies, Sesame Street, Barney and others.

JAKKS also bought the Flying Colors business of Michigan-based Colorbok Paper Products. Flying Colors' products include activity sets, clay compound play sets and lunch boxes. Licensed characters include Warner Bros.' Looney Tunes, Mattel's Barbie and Sanrio's Hello Kitty.

Terms of the purchases were not disclosed.

Mattel, the world's largest toymaker (Hasbro is second), purchased software publisher The Learning Company through a $3.8 billion stock deal in 1999. Mattel's late 1999 profit shortfall was blamed, at least in part, on the acquisition.

According to the Associated Press, Mattel earnings fell 42 percent in the third quarter of 1999. Mattel said it earned $135.3 million, or 32 cents per share on sales of $1.83 billion.

During 1998's third quarter, Mattel earned $233.8 million or 54 cents per share on sales of $1.88 billion. Including after-tax charges of $65 million, Mattel had a net income of $168.7 million for the 1998 quarter.

The Learning Company had been expected to bring a $50 million profit through the sale of software titles like Carmen Sandiego, American Greetings and Myst.

"While we are most disappointed in developments at The Learning Company, and by continuing difficulties in international markets, we are encouraged by U.S. sales increases in the quarter for our core Barbie, Fisher-Price, Hot Wheels and American Girl brands," Jill Barad, Mattel's chairman and chief executive officer, said in a news release.

Barad told the AP that there are no plans to sell The Learning Company, or change its management. She said she expected The Learning Company to return to profitability in 2000. She added the software maker planned to release several promising new titles, including one based on the immensely-popular Pokémon cartoon characters.

Barad noted that, "We've faced challenges before, and we are up to the challenges that are ahead of us."

> "... Hasbro felt they didn't have the right products or connections [to make money in the hobby game market]; now they do."
>
> — Peter Adkison
> *Wizards of the Coast president*

> "We've faced challenges before, and we are up to the challenges that are ahead of us."
>
> —Jill Barad
> *Mattel chairman, chief executive officer*

Auction Action

Barbie, Robot Among Record Setters in 1999

By Mike Jacquart

Star Wars and *Star Trek* toys might be all the rage these days, but 1950s-1960s space toys steal center stage when they come to auction.

Case in point, the Machine Man robot. The highly-coveted, ultra-rare Japanese Machine Man sold for a record $47,242 at a late summer 1999 auction held by Christie's South Kensington in London.

The astounding price topped even the $42,550 that Machine Man realized at a 1996 Sotheby's auction. Why the high price? The 15-inch Machine Man is one of the acclaimed Gang of Five, the rarest and tallest toy robots. And the battery-operated Machine Man, one of three known to exist (there are no known boxes), is the rarest of these rare toys. All five robots were made by Masudaya in the 1950s.

Other toy robots sold for more affordable prices at the Christie's sale. They included a Yonezawa Winkie Robot from the 1950s, $635; a Yonezawa Talking Robot, $363; and a Horikawa Machine Robot, $690.

Want a rare and unusual space-related item? A 54-inch Italian robot bubble gum dispenser, complete with electrically-lit eyes, brought $1,725;

RIGHT: The highly-coveted, ultra-rare Japanese Machine Man robot sold for a record $47,242 at an auction held by Christie's South Kensington in London. The astounding price topped even the $42,550 the Machine Man realized at a 1996 Sotheby's auction.

and *Space: 1999* Brian the Brain, a prototype of the robot/computer used in the Gerry Anderson TV series, realized $400.

Star Wars items were also offered. They included posters from Lucasfilm/Twentieth Century Fox that sold for around $180 each.

Other Characters

Mattel's Major Matt Mason line from the late 1960s to early 1970s is extremely collectible, so it was no surprise that a Major Matt Lunar Command set was one of the top sellers ($1,132) at a Toy Scouts sale. Another space enthusiast paid $600 for a Marx Operation Moonbase play set.

Actually, toys based on just about any TV or movie character from the 1950s-1960s will draw interest at auction. Toy Scouts' 1998 offerings also included an Irwin Beany & Cecil Leakin' Lena boat from 1962 that realized $303.

The Christie's South Kensington sale offered a rare Gilbert James Bond Spy Watch for $1,090; a Scalextric 007 James Bond set for $2,180; and a Dinky Jaguar based on *The New Avengers* TV series, $3,816.

Hopalong Cassidy collectors were treated to a rare gun-and-holster set at an auction held by the International Toy Collectors Association (ITCA).

The set, which sold for $2,700,

The legs had been repaired, but a Lionel Mickey and Minnie Hand Car still sold for $1,265 at an International Toy Collectors Association (ITCA) auction.

included never-fired revolvers and never-worn spurs. Only slight box damage detracted from this otherwise pristine piece.

No matter what your television favorite from yesteryear, chances are a TV Toyland auction offered something for you. Remember the Moonman from *The Bullwinkle Show*? An 8-inch vinyl Moonman figure was the top seller, topping its presale estimate by realizing $2,013.

Other leading sellers included an *H.R. Pufnstuf* Witchie Poo doll in Mint condition, $1,384; Charlie's Angels belt buckle, $905; Lost in Space robot that speaks Spanish, $1,200; Ideal Starsky & Hutch racing set, $706; vinyl Sherman (*The Bullwinkle Show*) figure, $699; and a vinyl Bullwinkle figure, $1,514.

While wonderful toys always turn up at Just Kids Nostalgia auctions, a number of colorful posters and lobby cards also brought exception prices at a Just Kids sale. Top sellers included a Ziegfeld Follies one-sheet poster from the 1920s, $5,191; a *Wizard of Oz* lobby card set from 1949 (a reissue), $5,024; and two colorful Lionel train posters from the 1950s that brought over $2,000 each.

Super Prices for Superheroes

Toys based on 1960s heroes were featured at

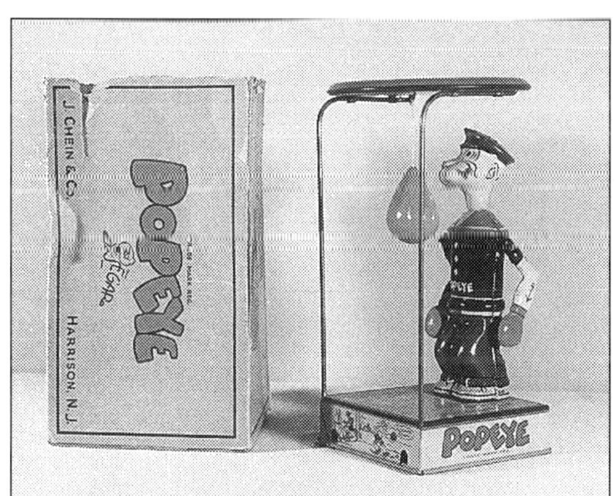

A Popeye with Punching Bag by Chein was the top seller at an ITCA sale, realizing $5,445.

Toy Scouts' fifth-annual superhero auction. But of all the neat toys on hand, it was a piece of original comic art — the 1966 cover from *Spider-Man #40* — that brought the auction's top bid. The piece fell within its presale estimate by bringing $21,000.

Other Spider-Man memorabilia included a reading motivation kit, $425; Spider-Man Halloween costume, $40; Spidey wedding pin, $40; and a flasher ring, $40.

Prefer Batman? A coloring book brought $30, the Batmobile from Mattel's Switch-N-Go set realized $110, a ceramic bank brought $179, a Marx Batcraft sold for $550 and a figural lamp realized $179.

Superman fans at the Toy Scouts sale could choose from lots like a rare wood-jointed doll, $1,485; and even oddball items like wallpaper, $75; and a muscle building certificate, $30.

Other items included a Mint in Package Aurora Green Hornet Black Beauty model kit, $750; Hawkman button, $65 — and even an ultra-rare Ideal Wonder Woman Super Queen doll, $800.

Lots of terrific Batman toys were featured at a Just Kids Nostalgia sale. The Bat-collectibles were from the

Prewar Disney toys, especially ultra-rare ones like this Mickey Cyclist and Pluto, always seem to fare well at auction. This toy, thought to be the only one in its original box, brought $12,000 at an International Toy Collectors Association (ITCA) auction.

ABOVE: In a major sale full of many highlights, this George Brown Walking Doll With Hoops was the biggest seller at a Sotheby's sale featuring the collection of the late Carol Andersen. The toy sold for $29,900. BELOW: As well as Barbies and antique dolls, 1960s and 1970s dolls and action figures are also turning up at auction. This G.I. Joe Imperial Soldier, part of Hasbro's 1960s Action Soldiers of the World line, brought $225 at a McMasters auction.

Lehmann's Lo & Li from the 1920s topped its presale estimate at the big Sotheby's sale by realizing $21,850.

collection of the late John McGonagle, one of Just Kids' first customers in 1978.

Batman memorabilia was led by a Remco plastic figure from 1970s that sold for $1,323. The 12-inch figure climbed walls with a grappling hook. It was in Mint in Package condition.

Another leading seller was an 8-inch Mego Bruce Wayne figure from 1974 that brought $1,058. The Montgomery Ward exclusive was dressed in a gray suit, with a blue tie and black shoes.

Rare Batman play sets also brought four-digit prices. An Ideal set originally sold at Sears in 1966 realized $1,205, and a 1966 Remco Gotham City set brought $1,103.

Also at the Just Kids sale, a Corgi Crime Busters gift set from 1966 — it included a Batmobile, Batboat, *Man From U.N.C.L.E.* car and a James Bond Aston Martin — brought $1,035.

While Batman memorabilia was the highlight of the auction, plenty of other interesting items were also available. A rare Mego *Planet of the Apes* action figure in a Japanese box brought $1,048, and an *Apes* play set realized $457.

Want still more evidence that play sets in their original boxes are in demand with collectors? A *Voyage to the Bottom of the Sea* set sold for $1,522. The 1960s Remco toy, based on the TV series, featured a window box with an underwater diorama.

Plenty of Popeye

Lots of Popeye toys

in pristine shape dropped anchor at Bill Bertoia Auctions' October Toy Fest Sale in Philadelphia.

Hoge's Popeye Speedboat was the auction's leading seller. The white-and-green lithographed pressed steel boat fell within its presale estimate by realizing $18,150. The rare boat, one of three known to exist, depicts a tin Popeye seated at the wheel of the 15-inch boat. A large clockwork activates the mechanism of this extremely elusive toy.

But this item was hardly the only pristine Popeye toy offered. A similar toy, a Hoge Popeye the Sailor in

ABOVE: Think toy vehicle collectors are only interested in Mattel Hot Wheels cars? A 24-inch Buddy L Red Baby truck in Near Mint condition was the top-selling vehicle at Bertoia's A Century of Toys Sale. It brought $22,000 — triple its presale estimate. BELOW: An American National Packard convertible realized $11,000 at the Bertoia auction.

Rowboat from 1935 exceeded its presale estimate by selling for $9,900.

Linemar toys featuring everyone's favorite sailor included a Popeye Basketball Player, $2,750; Popeye & Brutus Boxers, $1,760; Smoking Popeye, $4,400; Popeye Tank (similar to a Superman toy from the same period), $275; and Wimpy on Trike, $1,045.

A Popeye with Punching Bag by Chein was the top seller at an International Toy Collectors Association (ITCA) auction, realizing $5,445. A Marx Bubble Blowing Popeye brought $853.

Mickey Remains Disney's Star

It's clear that, for many collectors, collectible is spelled M-I-C-K-E-Y M-O-U-S-E.

Want proof? Mickey Mouse's first book signed by Walt Disney topped its lofty presale estimate by bringing $5,724 at a 'Tiques auction. The book contained wonderful graphics, especially the back page that features Noah's Ark Disney characters.

Other top-selling Disney lots included an 8-inch Steiff Mickey Mouse doll from the 1930s, $2,200; a 1932 Mickey counter-top game — they're extremely rare since Disney destroyed them because it was considered gambling — $1,985; an aluminum Mickey radiator cap from France to adorn your vintage car, $475; 6-inch tin-lithographed mechanical toy of Mickey playing the saxophone, $2,804; 7-inch crawling celluloid Donald Duck, $1,190; 7-inch 1934 Donald Duck celluloid roly poly, $1,190; Emerson Snow White radio, $2,350; Mickey wood watch display, $2,340; and a rare 1930s Minnie Mouse hood ornament, $4,375.

A 9-1/2-inch composition Mickey Mouse cowboy by Knickerbocker, made only in 1936, sold for an auction-leading $12,100 at an ITCA sale.

Mickey also raised a fuss at several ITCA auctions. This 500-lot sale offered the Mickey Cyclist and Pluto still in its original box. As legend has it, this colorful Mickey Mouse toy was introduced in the 1930s, but production ceased shortly thereafter due to its fragile construction. The celluloid Pluto was connected to the tricycle only by a small hole in his foot which was easily broken when handled.

Due to numerous complaints from customers about its weak construction, the toy was redesigned. Mickey ended up seated on the tricycle, while Pluto was left out. Mickey Cyclist and Pluto has only surfaced a few times, and the one at the ITCA sale might be the only one known in its original box. No wonder it brought an auction-leading $12,000!

At a different ITCA auction, a Fun-E-Flex Mickey figure by the George Borgfeldt company sold for $2,860, and a Lionel Mickey and Minnie Hand Car brought $1,265 despite the fact that the toy's legs had been repaired.

A prewar Disney toy also turned up at a Sotheby's sale. A Mickey Mouse Hurdy-Gurdy from the 1930s brought $4,600.

Beatles, Elvis Reign

Pearl Jam? The Wallflowers?

RIGHT: The pressed steel Popeye Sailor in Rowboat, made by Hoge in the 1930s, sold for $9,900. The clockwork mechanism activiates the rowing motion of this pressed steel toy. The tin-lithographed Popeye is seated at the wheel of the speedboat.

LEFT: Well, blow me down, Popeye toys were big in 1999. A Hoge Popeye Speedboat realized an auction-leading $18,150 at a Bill Bertoia sale. The item, one of only three known, depicts a tin-lithographed Popeye at the wheel of a speedboat. A large clockwork key activates the mechanism.

Forget current groups. When it comes to rock and roll collectibles there's nothing like Beatles and Elvis memorabilia.

Only about 5,000 Beatles record players were produced in the 1960s, so it's no surprise that a Fab Four enthusiast shelled out $5,500 for a specimen in Excellent to Mint condition at a 'Tiques auction. The winning bidder paid more than double the presale estimate.

Music lovers took home additional items such as a 1956 Elvis sneaker box, $1,056; a Beatles *Yellow Submarine* promotional poster, $345; a set of four *Yellow Submarine* banks from 1968, $2,739; and an Elvis zippered binder from 1956, $1,495.

Prewar Toys are Still Big

While toys featuring characters like Mickey, Elvis or the Beatles grab a lot of headlines, just about any prewar toy in pristine condition — especially those from noted manufacturers like Lehmann, Ives, Schoenhut and George Brown, bring good prices.

The top seller at a Sotheby's auction was a George Brown Walking Doll With Hoops that fetched $29,900. This rare toy, patented in 1872, features a composition doll pushing two oversized wheels centering a clockwork mechanism, bell and a boy. When wound, the doll walks forward, and the figure rocks back and forth as the bell rings.

The sale, which featured the estate of the late Carol Andersen, included numerous prewar toys that brought five-figure prices.

The extremely rare boxed Lehmann Lo & Li sold for $21,850. This rare toy from the late 1920s features the jolly musicians, Lo, the clown who plays the accordion, and Li, the top-hatted dancer.

An Ives mechanical Sewing Machine Girl realized $18,400. The toy, patented in 1875, features a china head doll seated at a sewing machine. It was formerly in the Perelman Toy Museum.

A Bergmann clockwork Girl On Bicycle sold for $14,950. This piece, patented in 1877, features a composition doll atop a tin-plated bicycle balanced on a metal ring. When wound, the cyclist speeds around the circle.

A menagerie of Schoenhut lots at the Sotheby's sale was highlighted by two of the rarest toys the firm ever produced. Teddy's Adventures in Africa was introduced shortly after Teddy Roosevelt's trip to that continent. It was in the original box and included a wood-jointed Teddy; a photographer modeled after the Rough Rider's son, Kermit; a glass-eyed rhinoceros; lion; deer and jungle-printed background. The item realized $19,550.

Going to the circus used to be a much bigger deal than it is today, and Schoenhut captured the flair of that

ABOVE: An extremely rare French bisque artist doll by Albert Marque was sold by Theriault's for $135,000. This was a new record for a 20th-century French doll. BELOW: Selling well beyond its presale estimate at $33,000 was this rare and exquisite Jumeau.

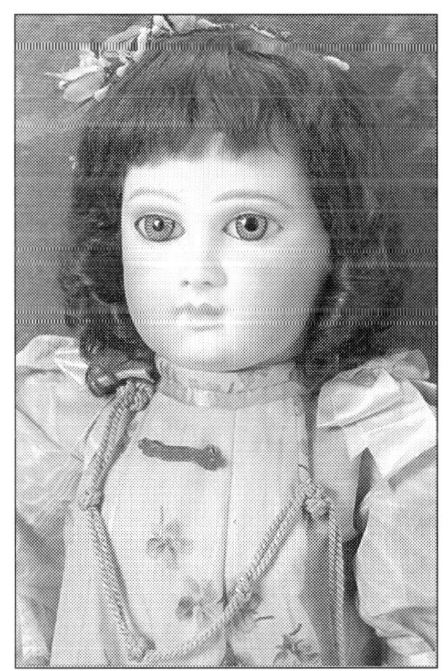

era with the rare oval Humpty Dumpty Circus Tent. It came with two colorful side banners depicting a bustling circus scene featuring banners of the side show attractions, including The Beautiful Snake Charmer and The Strongest Man on Earth. It carried a presale estimate of $4,000 to $6,000 and realized $17,250.

More Stunning Prewar Prices

Mechanical and still banks are among the featured items at most Bill Bertoia auctions, and the October Toy Fest Sale was no exception.

A J&E Stevens Calamity Bank and a Stevens Multiplying Bank each brought $12,100. A Stevens Horse Race sold for $11,500, and a Kyser & Rex Mammy & Child that realized $10,450.

A number of prewar cast-iron miniature stoves brought exceptional prices, led by an impressively-detailed Majestic Stove Co. sample in pristine condition that brought $15,950.

Bertoia's A Century of Toys Sale was anchored by the incredible

ABOVE: Looking for something unusual to add to your doll collection? McMasters' Cherished Companions auction included a Buster Brown Rolly doll, $590; a 14-inch Schoenhut Rolly Doll, $800; a Schoenhut doll house, $1,150; and a Schoenhut carved hair boy, $1,300. BELOW: An 18-inch Kestner doll sold for $5,200 at a different McMasters doll auction.

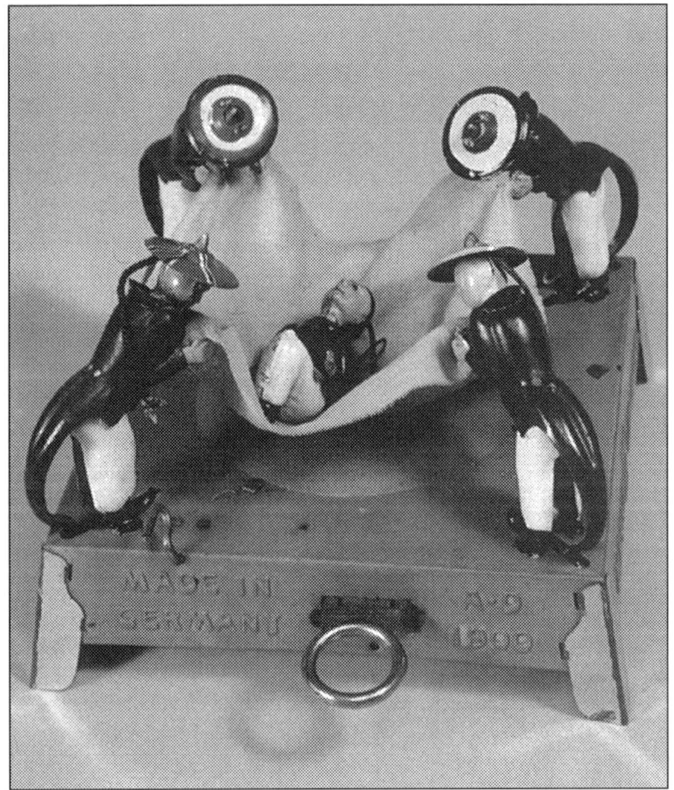

The rare Lehmann Boxer brought a whopping $27,500 at a Bill Bertoia auction. The toy is based on the secret "Boxer" society created during the occupation of China during the 1900s.

collection of longtime collector Bob Lyons of Ypsilanti, Mich., the important Lehmann collection of John and Adrianne Haley and the extensive biscuit tin collection of Stuart and Linda Cropper.

The top seller was a German tin-lithographed eight-man scull with coxswain that sold for $28,600. Its presale estimate was only $6,000 to $8,000! The 27-inch toy featured a clockwork mechanism and small disc wheels for forward motions.

An extremely rare Lehmann Boxer exceeded its whopping $16,000 to $21,000 presale estimate by bringing $27,500.

The clockwork toy — based on the secret "Boxer" society created during the occupation of China during the 1900s — featured hand-painted Chinese figures and a fabric blanket.

Ives enthusiasts likely went ga-ga over an 1870s mechanical horse with a whipping driver. The toy featured an intricate clockwork mechanism that caused the boy to whip the horse into apparent flight. The rare Ives toy fell within its lofty presale estimate by selling for $24,200.

The popularity of colorful, tin lithographed items was evidenced again when Gray Dunn's Racing Car Biscuit sold for $20,900. The rare English car featured a bright yellow-and-red color scheme, disc wheels and a tin driver.

Vintage Vehicles

Hot Wheels may be cool, and Matchbox might be better known. But it's clear collectors haven't forgotten about prewar vehicles made of pressed steel, cast-iron and lithographed tin.

A 24-inch Buddy "L" Red Baby truck in Near Mint condition was the top selling vehicle at Bertoia's A Century of Toys Sale. This finely-preserved toy sold for $22,000 — triple its presale estimate!

Other top-selling vehicles included a Packard, $17,600 and a Packard convertible, $11,000, both by the American National Co.; Buddy "L" Junior City Dray truck, $7,425; Kingsbury motor-driven truck, $5,225; and a rare hand-painted steam powered Indian motor-cycle, $12,100.

Meanwhile, a pair of Arcade cast-iron moving vans were among the top sellers at Bertoia's October Toy Fest Sale. A model with the "Lammerts Furniture" inscription on both sides with a silver grille and bumper, nick-eled driver and disc wheels and hinged rear doors brought $15,400. An "Edelen" orange van with spare tires mounted to side panels sold for $13,200. Both were within the toys' lofty presale estimates.

But a Marklin New York battleship grabbed the highest bid among vehicle lots, selling for an eye-popping $16,500. The restored ship was hand-painted and included four lifeboats, cannons and turrets, masts and a crow's nest. It measured 35 inches long and was steam powered.

Doepke enthusiasts were treated to a spotlight truck that brought $1,450 at an ITCA auction.

Bears and Barbies

Even non-collectors are familiar with the outstanding prices that Steiff bears can bring. But did you know that Steiff makes other plush animals which can also bring great prices?

A rare set of Skittles from the early 20th century, which included a bear majestically dressed as a king, an elephant, dog, pig, monkey, cat, rabbit and sheep, all with Steiff's trademark buttons in ear, brought $17,250 at a Sotheby's auction. The amount was nearly triple the presale estimate.

A collector paid a record auction price for a Barbie at a Theriault's sale. Theriault's is known for its outstanding doll auctions, and the East Coast firm did not disappoint as an extremely rare 1959 Ponytail Barbie #1 in a rare Barbie-Q outfit and its original box sold for $13,500.

Theriault's also offered a 1960 Ponytail Barbie #3 with box for $4,400 and a 1960 Mix-and-Match play set that realized $2,600.

A Ponytail Barbie #1, brunette, was the top seller at McMasters' Autumn Splendor sale. The doll, from 1960, realized $2,700. The value of early Barbies like these was apparent, as the doll brought the auction's top price despite slightly fuzzy hair, a protruding cylinder on her left foot, a worn booklet and a box that was in Poor condition.

Demand for early Barbies was evidenced at McMasters' Twist and Shout auction. A Ponytail Barbie #2, brunette, was

A rare Ponytail Barbie #1 in a rare Barbie-Q outfit, complete with accessories and original box, brought $13,500 at a Theriault's auction — a new record for a Mattel Barbie doll!

the top seller, realizing $2,600 despite flaws that included many loose hair strands, a deteriorated rubber band, a lighter flesh tone on the arms, back and back of legs than elsewhere on the doll. The Barbie wore a Gay Parisienne dress.

Other Dolls

Highlighting a Theriault's Century Remembered sale was an extremely rare French bisque artist doll by Albert Marque with its original signed costume.

The doll, once owned by the French Lumiere family, famous for having invented the motion picture, brought $135,000 — a record for a 20th century French doll.

Theriault's also offered an exquisite French bisque portrait bebe by Jumeau with unusual plump modeling which sold for $33,000, well exceeding its $15,000 to $20,000 presale estimate.

Perhaps the most unusual item at the Theriault's auction was a rare

The oval Humpty Dumpty Circus Tent was the largest toy circus tent Schoenhut ever produced. It featured colorful banners and side show attractions, including The Beautiful Snake Charmer and The Strongest Man on Earth. This rare toy realized $17,250 at a Sotheby's auction.

French porcelain Surprise doll whose skirt would open to reveal a kitchen. Theriault's sold this doll for $13,500 — over six times the presale estimate.

"The Glamour of Childhood Days, Alexander's Elegant Ladies," was a Theriault's auction devoted to the fashion dolls of Madame Alexander.

Highlighting this sale was a classic and exquisite Alexander model of the Lady in red which brought $3,100. Other notable fashion models included "A Child's Dream Come True," probably the most lavish of the bridal gowns with a cap variation. It realized $2,600. A Renoir Cissy with vivid colors and a fabulous hat brought $3,000.

The smaller, 10-inch Madame Alexanders included a white satin Margot that brought $800.

An antique Continental porcelain head doll with kid leather body led all

doll lots at a Phillips-Selkirk auction. It realized $1,200.

Over 200 avid doll collectors participaed in McMasters' "Everything's Coming Up Daisies," auction. Participants raised their paddles in anticipation of owning a fabulous doll from the second part of Lucia Kirsch's collection, or with the hopes of going home with a beautiful Jumeau, Steiner or a Schoenhut.

Astounding all in attendance was a lovely 27-inch Heinrich Handwerck that realized an amazing $2,500; a 24-inch Simon & Halbig 1159 Lady with brown sleep eyes and real lashes that brought $3,200 and a 15-inch Kammer & Reinhardt 115A Baby that brought $3,900.

Jumeaus were in full bloom with a 20-inch Tete picked up by an auction attendee for a whopping $3,700 and a 17-inch Fashion Lady that brought an amazing $3,000.

An array of toys with moving parts was also offered. A Schoenhut Bungalow with a raising roof and two exterior walls that swing open went for a smashing $1,050; and a Stubborn Donkey tin wind-up carted his way home for $355.

Georgene Novelties grew to great

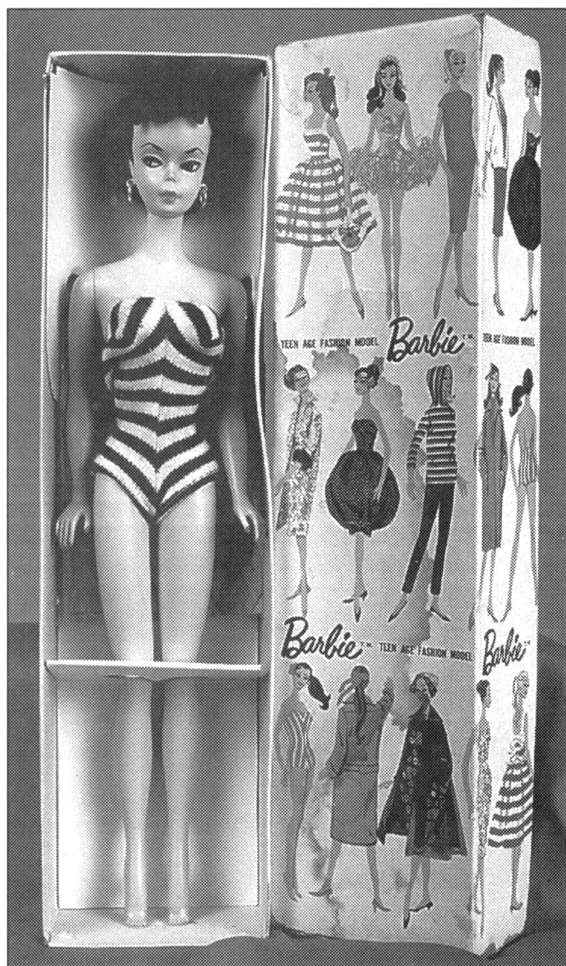

LEFT: A Ponytail Barbie #1, brunette, was the top seller at McMasters' Autumn Splendor sale. The doll, from 1960, realized $2,700.

heights with Mint in Box samples of comic characters Becassine, Tubby Tom, Nancy and Sluggo realizing between $775 and $925 each.

More Dolls at Theriault's

Early rare dolls and collectible 20th-century dolls were both offered at Theriault's sale. A previously undocumented German bisque character doll, circa 1910, by Bawo and Dotter, a firm better known for its 1880s black-haired china dolls, sold for a strong $19,500.

The sum of $15,500 was the final selling price of an 1840s wooden-bodied 19-inch china doll with exposed ears, while its sister doll, with more modestly curl-covered ears, topped at $5,000. A petite size Bru bebe also sold for that price.

Another French dolls included a bisque bebe by Jules Steiner that brought $9,500.

Proliferation of Online Sales

Perhaps the biggest change in the auction business in recent years is the continued growth of online auctions. While online auctions are a daily occurrence — especially with online services such as eBay — here are a number of the highlights from 1999.

One hundred-five bids were

The sum of $15,500 was Theriault's final selling price of an 1840s-era wooden-bodied 19-inch china doll with exposed ears, while its sister doll, with more modestly curl-covered ears, topped at $5,000.

Auction Advice

Buying at auctions can be a fun, challenging and interesting way to acquire those treasured toys you desire. But if you're not familiar with how auctions are run, you may want to keep some tips in mind. Being informed will allow you to make smarter bids and get more satisfying results.

• **Examine the merchandise and ask questions**. Of course this isn't possible in phone, mail or online auctions, but it is possible to find out about an auctioneer's reputation. Ask others, was the "Mint" item actually in Mint condition? Ask a lot of questions about the item you'll be bidding on to avoid future regret or hassles.

• **Ask for photos** if they're available. If you're attending an auction, examine the condition of items and scout the competition. As you attend more auctions, you'll recognize some of the same faces and get a better handle on what particular people will be bidding on.

• **Register early**. To avoid tying up bidding lines, register early — even the night before if possible. For phone auctions, don't call at the final hour if you haven't already registered.

• **Bid wisely**. Don't open with an outrageously high bid — if you're the only bidder you may end up paying too much. But also don't open with a laughably low bid either, you may not be taken seriously. Become familiar with presale estimates if they're offered.

• **Honor your bid**. If your bid wins, you've bought the piece — simple as that, right? It may sound elementary, but too often auctioneers are stiffed by bidders who don't pick up or pay for items. It's a sure way to ruin future relationships with auction houses.

received on eBay for a specially-designed Hot Wheels desk. But, like any auction, only one bidder — with a bid of $25,103 — was lucky enough to win the item.

Talk show hostess Rosie O'Donnell donated the one-of-a-kind desk, which contained approximately 100 die-cast Hot Wheels vehicles.

The desk, created by chief Hot Wheels designer Larry Wood, featured an aluminum top with a working track set and shift lever to launch Mattel Hot Wheels cars.

Hot Wheels in the desk included a rare 1998 Christmas Dairy Delivery truck. The truck was made as a gift for Hot Wheels designers and has never been on sale.

Collectors have placed its value at around $2,000.

Hasbro's online charity auction — a kickoff celebration for its launch of *HasbroCollectors.com* — ended with the highest bids placed on one-of-a-kind collectibles such as a G.I. Joe figure done in the winning bidder's likeness, the 1999 line of 3-3/4-inch *Star Wars: Episode I* action figures and an autographed Starting Lineups Mark McGwire figure.

The highest bid featured went for the personalized G.I. Joe. It sold for $2,951, while a signed G.I. Joe Colin Powell figure brought $960.

The 1999 line of 3-3/4-inch *Star Wars* figures (50 figures) went for $2,750, while the signed McGwire figure realized $915.

All proceeds from the auction — more than $13,000 — went to the Hasbro Children's Hospital in Providence, R.I.

A Ty Beanie Baby — specifically, a limited-edition (253) #1 bear — realized a whopping $12,000 in an online auction. The red bears were only issued to Ty salesmen.

Taking Terrific Photos

Great Toy Shots are Easy With These Tips

Photographs are perhaps the most captivating part of any book or magazine. They allow readers to see what often is impossible to express in words. That's especially true for pictures of toys.

Without a photograph, it's difficult to grasp the true sheen and beauty of tin lithography, the color of Ponytail Barbie #1's eyes, or even the condition of a game box. Those intricacies are important to the discerning collector.

Shots of individual toys usually bring at least acceptable results.

You Don't Have to Be a Pro

While many photos that appear in *Toy Shop* are professionally shot, many others are photographed and submitted by readers, collectors and dealers.

If you're planning to submit photos to a magazine (or if you just want

Do . . .

• Pick a film for the type of shooting you'll be doing — color, slide, or print. Slides are best for submitting color shots to a magazine. Print film is best for enlargements and for use in newspapers.

• Select the proper speed of film. An ASA of 50 or 100 works well because the image will hold up better when magnified.

• Use a plain background. Setting up a toy on a patterned or busy background distracts from the focal point. Gray is a neutral background color that can really make a toy stand out.

• It may sound elementary, but make sure the toy is in focus, especially important details on the piece or box.

• Shoot extra frames of your subject. This way you'll have a back-up in case one gets lost or destroyed. Shoot various angles of your toy: top, bottom, front, sides, or other angles.

• Shooting from different angles can also better disperse light, eliminating unwanted glare on the subject.

• When shooting, always use an F-stop between 32-16 for maximum depth of field. If possible, mount your camera on a tripod. Steady shots make great enlargements and slides.

• Identify prints, by information either on a separate sheet or on the back of the print. When writing on the back, however, do so lightly to avoid damaging the image or use a taped label or self-stick note.

• Take individual shots whenever possible as opposed to group shots. Group shots can turn out fine, but individual shots better ensure success, especially for novice photographers.

. . . Don't

• Don't have people or pets in the picture if you plan to submit the photo to a magazine. Nothing spoils a shot more than unwanted distractions.

• Don't get so close that your reflection appears in the subject you're photographing.

• Don't photograph the toy on a patterned or same-color background.

• Don't cut off part of the toy when framing the shot.

• When handling prints, don't paperclip photos; this may scratch the image.

• For photos to be used for editorial purposes, don't cut the image of the toy from the print. Send the entire photo.

• Don't stand far away. Remember, your camera isn't a telescope. When in doubt, stand as close to the subject matter as possible while still keeping the subject in focus.

Going to a toy or other collectibles show? Editors love to see shots of brightly-colored displays like this Texaco sign.

photos for insurance or inventory purposes), several tips can help you produce the best results.

See the accompanying do's and don'ts lists for advice on photographing your toys.

You Know What You Like

Remember: Think of what you look for in magazine photos. You want to be able to identify a toy easily and see its key attributes (color, shape, size, etc.) without distracting elements like shadow, glare or busy backgrounds. Toys arc fun, and photographing them can be too with a little practice.

Thanks to Krause Publications' Staff Photographer Ross Hubbard for his help with this article. Hubbard spends much of his time photographing everything from vintage cars and old coins to toys and collectible weapons. Many of the cover photos on "Toy Shop" and other Krause magazines (and the cover of this annual) are the result of the talent and efforts of both Hubbard and fellow Krause photographer Kris Kandler.

ABOVE, BELOW: Whenever possible, photograph different angles of the same toy.

While this photo is in focus and gives a reader an idea the types of toys that were available a a given show, it lacks the focus on a specific subject matter that editors typically look for. Individual photos of items like the Allied Van Lines truck or the Snoopy toy would have turned out better.

For Top Photos, Equipment Counts

You don't have to be a professional photographer or even have expensive equipment to take a good photograph. But the type of equipment you use can make a difference in the quality of your pictures. Here are some photography basics to consider.

Type of Film	Characteristics
Black and white	Easy to work with; best for newspapers.
Color print	Fairly easy to work with. Some adjustments can be made.
Color slide	Best color reproduction, but hard to work with.

Speed of Film	Characteristics
Slow (25-200 ASA)	Less grain, big enlargements. Use outdoors with plenty of light.
Fast (400-3,200ASA)	More grain. Use indoors; can be used in low light.

Flash	Characteristics
Use if needed	Adds necessary light indoors; also fills in outdoors shadows.

Camera	Characteristics
35mm Single Lens Reflex	Most flexible format; some experience needed
35mm Point and Shoot	Takes acceptable images

Lenses	Characteristics
50mm	Good standard lens
28-80	Zoom; good all-around lens
55mm Macro	Good for close-ups
105mm Macro	Good for close-ups

Talking Toys

Technology Leads to More Interactive Toys

By Mike Jacquart

Whether one wants to call them high-tech toys, tech toys, interactive toys or just plain talking toys, it's clear that more and more toys that "say and do things" are being produced.

Increasing numbers of talking toys should not be seen as a surprise in this technological day and age, but talking toys are not new.

"This is something that has evolved in the industry over the years," said Diane Cardinale, assistant communications director with the

Toy Manufacturers of America.

Indeed. Remember Teddy Ruxpin? Or how about Mattel's talking Casper the Friendly Ghost or Chatty Cathy from the 1960s?

Actually, talking toys date as far back as a talking doll developed by Thomas Edison in 1878, according to

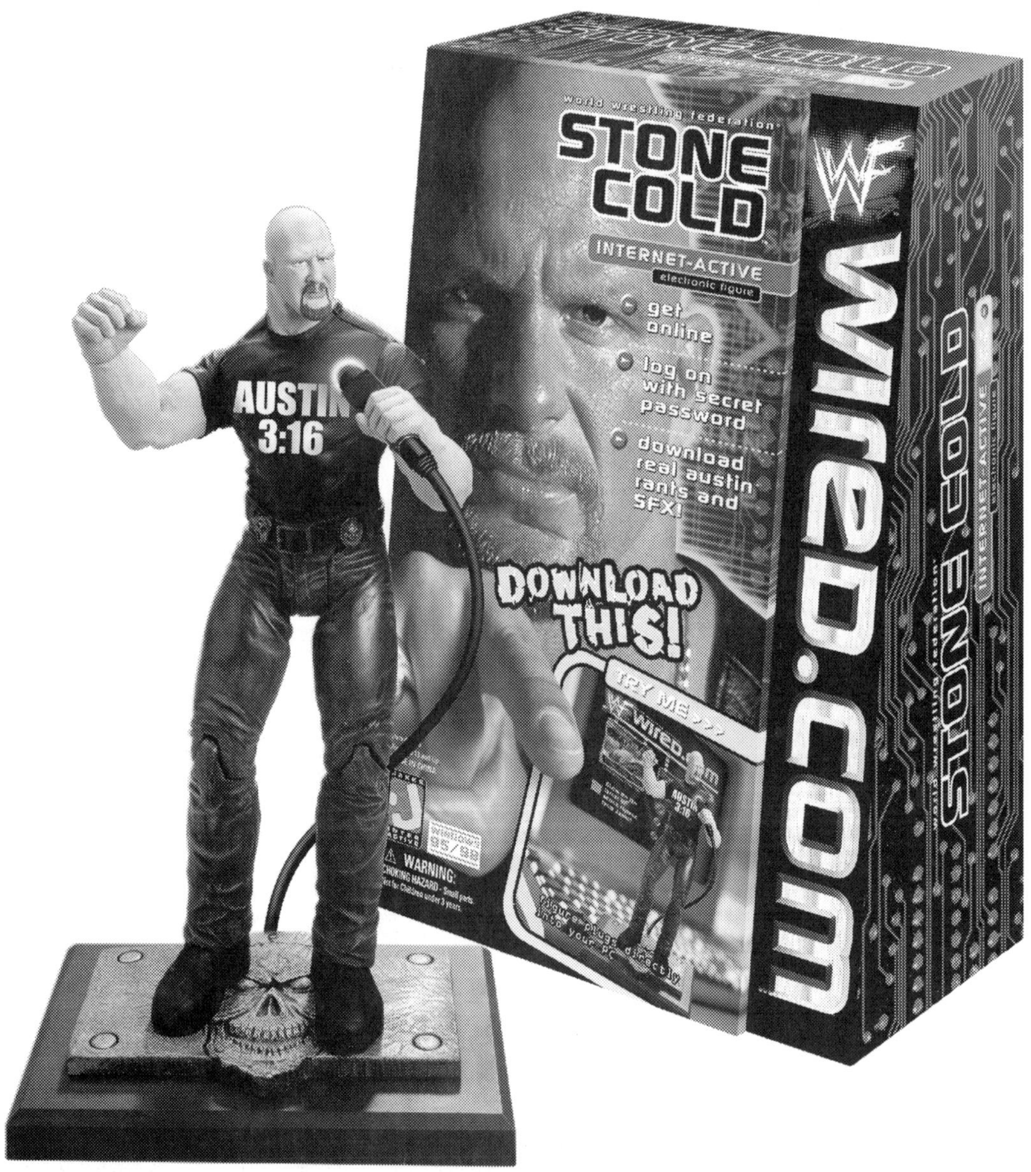

ABOVE: Today's talking toys feature technology that's much more sophisticated than simple pullstring mechanisms. Consider JAKKS Pacific's Stone Cold Steve Austin 12-inch figures that can download phrases from the World Wrestling Federation's web site at www.wwfwired.com.

If Gibson Greetings' Silly Slammers didn't talk they'd be just one of the many plush toy lines around. But the funny phrases they say when dropped or "slammed" make these toys unique.

Kathy and Don Lewis, authors of *Talking Toys of the 20th Century* (1999, Collector Books).

It seems that Edison, inventor of the phonograph, used a voice activated crank that protruded from the doll's back.

"Due to the delicate mechanism and the vast amount of non-working dolls, the production ceased in 1890," the Lewises wrote in their book.

But while toys that talk are not new, it's also clear that today's playthings have come a long way since dolls with pullstrings that recited a few phrases, and that was it.

Talking Toys Get Sophisticated

In fact, one could make a case that some toy companies would not even be in business if not for recent breakthroughs in technology.

Consider Thinkway Toys, makers of *Star Wars* interactive talking banks. Darth Vader came to gloriously evil life in a 1997 bank. Push the button, and Vader's ominous theme music plays as he wields his saber. Then Vader's voice reverberates as he declares, "Impressive. Most impressive. But you are not a Jedi yet."

The same year, Thinkway issued C-3PO and R2-D2 talking banks. "Threepio," as he's called, declares, "I'm C-3PO, human cyborg relations, and this is my counterpart R2-D2."

Thinkway released *Star Wars: Episode I* Qui-Gon Jinn, Darth Maul and Obi-Wan Kenobi interactive talking banks in 1999. The banks work individually as well as interactively.

Each character performs different moves. In fact, snap all three of them together, and they perform a final duel between both the good (Obi-Wan and Qui-Gon) and evil (Maul) sides of the Force. "Be wary. I sense a disturbance in the Force," says Qui-Gon Jinn. "It's the Jedi!" declares Darth Maul. "I feel it also Master," states Obi-Wan Kenobi.

It's enough to make a toy fan feel that they're watching *Star Wars: Episode I The Phantom Menace* in the theater for the umpteenth time.

Hasbro's Furby is another of the talking toys that do much more than talking toys from earlier decades.

Talking Figures

In addition, Hasbro's 3-3/4-inch *Episode I* action figures issued in 1999 came with a computer chip that allowed them to talk — provided one

Thinkway's "Episode I" Qui-Gon Jinn bank not only talks, but wields a light-saber as well.

purchased the comm tech reader (sold separately for about $20).

It seems that children and adults have different views about the toys.

"Most people thought they [the readers] were cool at first, but once the novelty wore off, they would rather ditch the chips for a cheaper retail price on the figures," said *Star Wars* collector Chris Fawcett.

"This is a collector view though," Fawcett stressed. "I would suspect that kids would get more value out of the chips than adult collectors."

Talking Beanbags

But *Star Wars* items aren't the only talking toys. Gibson Greetings' Silly Slammers, called America's first "beanbags with an attitude," are talking characters with outrageous expressions, bright colors and funny phrases. Each miniature beanbag blurts out a unique phrase when dropped or slammed.

"The number one feature [of Silly Slammers] is the sound element," stated Doug Guendel, Gibson's vice president and general manager of retail entertainment sales. (Gibson is mainly known for greeting cards, but

it got into the toy business with Silly Slammers in 1997).

Benefits of Technology

Cardinale noted that as technology has advanced and the cost of producing computer chips has decreased, it's become more cost effective for toy companies to make talking toys.

"The toy industry is just following what's going in the rest of the business world," she said. "It's always been that way — as technology goes, the toy industry follows."

Guendel agreed. While the first wave of Silly Slammers could only recite one phrase, Slammers issued since then can exclaim as many as four different phrases. Lights and sound effects have also been added to some of the beanbags.

"As the cost comes down, we've been able to add more sayings," Guendel said.

JAKKS Pacific President Stephen Berman agreed.

"As technology develops so quickly, we hope it'll allow an even lower price point in the future — although we believe we offer a very low price," Berman said.

While most, if not all, of Thinkway's and Gibson Greetings' toys talk, toy manufacturers like JAKKS Pacific and McFarlane Toys are more selective about the number of interactive toys they issue.

Not All Toys Should Talk

"I think it depends on the line," stated McFarlane Toys Communications Director Steve Hamady, about whether action figures will talk or not. "What we try to do is come out with a price point ($7.95 retail) that's about the same each time. We're not likely to see sound chips in a Spawn line because of our detail — we'd have to go [charge] $10.95. But if it fits, we'll do it."

And McFarlane's Austin Powers line, its lone talking action figures to date, clearly fit — although admittedly they meant more work.

"It's [talking action figures] definitely more work," Hamady stated. "Any time you add a step in the production process, you add more steps of approval."

For instance, Mike Myers, who portrayed Powers in the 1999 smash New Line Cinema

---

LEFT: McFarlane Toys, best known for its Spawn action figures, got into the talking toy market in 1999 with its Austin Powers line.

"God bless the space program. Without them [their technology], you wouldn't see nearly as much of this [making talking toys]."

—Steve Hamady
McFarlane Toys communications director

Snap Thinkway's "Episode I" banks together, and they perform a final duel between the good and evil sides of the Force. Photo courtesy Thinkway catalog.

movie *Austin Powers: The Spy Who Shagged Me,* had to approve the licensed talking figures before production could begin.

Still, the fact that even *some* talking figures are beginning to be produced by McFarlane is proof to Hamady how far technology has come in recent years.

"Sophisticated technology is the reason we're able to do this," he said. "Computers used to take up the space of a whole warehouse, so this [technology] is great for everyone.

"God bless the space program," Hamady added. "Without them, you wouldn't see nearly as much of this [making talking toys]."

Like McFarlane, Berman believes there has to be a unique application for talking toys to be good sellers.

It would appear JAKKS' interactive Stone Cold Steve Austin action figures deliver on the "unique" front. The figures feature technology that can download the wrestling superstar's actual phrases, challenges and comments from the World Wrestling Federation's web site located at *www.wwfwired.com.*

The Internet-active figures, which retail in the $40 to $50 range, come

with a microphone that lights up to inform the user that the figure is downloading.

"With the traffic [an estimated 150 million page views per month] on the WWF's web site, we believe it's [the figure] a win-win for both us and

"Board games alone are almost a $2 billion industry, so there's no fear that old toys will go away. At the same time, there's room for new toys."

—*Diane Cardinale*
Toy Manufacturers of America assistant communications director

them [the WWF]," Berman said. "But I don't believe you can do this with a generic toy," Berman stressed.

The Wired.Com figure line also comes with a "rant manager" CD-ROM that lets fans repeatedly create their own phrases using different words each time, as well as a membership number and 12 month admission to the WWF's web site, allow fans to access the sound bytes updated on the site.

And that's not all. JAKKS is also producing high-tech, 6-inch figures and play sets that feature sensors that activate personality-specific theme songs, lights and photographs of WWF superstars as they enter the TitanTRON Live play set.

JAKKS Pacific also plans to issue six additional Internet-active figures

in 2000.

"The Rock is one of the next WWF stars we'll do," Berman said.

While Berman is proud of the fact his firm is "ahead of the game" in the interactive toy market, toy officials stressed that while increasingly more sophisticated toys are the wave of the future, there's still room for traditional toys as well.

"Toys is a $21 billion industry," said Cardinale. "Board games alone are almost a $2 billion industry, so there's no fear that old toys will go away," she said. "At the same time, there's room for new toys."

Hamady agreed.

"It's [talking toys] not the trend for everybody."

ABOVE: *Hasbro's 3-3/4-inch "Star Wars: Episode I" action figures talked, provided one had the comm tech reader that sold separately for about $20. Photo courtesy Hasbro catalog. BELOW: Watto, one of the action figures in the line.*

Can't go to the wrestling match? JAKKS Pacific offers the next best thing with TitanTRON Live play sets that feature personality-specific theme songs, lights and photographs of WWF superstars as they enter the set.

Buying and Selling
Robots, Space Toys & Superheroes
Top Prices Paid
See our new updated web site: www.bergintoys.com
MARK BERGIN
Hundreds of Toys for Sale
mbergin@top.monad.net
Tel: (603) 924-2079   Fax: (603) 924-2022

WWW.UNIQUECOLLECTIBLES.COM

GENUINE HAND SIGNED & CERTIFIED COLOR 8"x10" PHOTOS

Gillian Anderson - $65
Jennifer Aniston - $50
Backstreet Boys - $150
Drew Barrymore - $50
Jessica Biel - $40
David Boreanaz - $35
Sandra Bullock - $50
Neve Campbell - $50
Laetitia Casta - $45
Cindy Crawford - $65
Tom Cruise - $95
Cameron Diaz - $50
Leonardo DiCaprio - $60
Shannen Doherty - $50
Carmen Electra - $50
Calista Flockhart - $45
Harrison Ford - $125

Rebecca Gayheart - $45
Mel Gibson - $110
Heather Graham - $40
Tom Hanks - $50
Melissa Joan Hart - $50
Salma Hayek - $50
Katie Holmes - $50
Jewel - $50
Angelina Jolie - $45
Catherine Zeta Jones - $50
Ashley Judd - $50
Nicole Kidman - $50
Heidi Klum - $45
Lucy Lawless - $50
Jennifer Lopez - $50
Madonna - $195
Ricky Martin - $45

Ewan McGregor - $50
Alyssa Milano - $50
Gwyneth Paltrow - $50
Natalie Portman - $50
Keanu Reeves - $50
Denise Richards - $45
Julia Roberts - $95
Keri Russell - $35
Meg Ryan - $60
Will Smith - $50
Spice Girls - $150
Uma Thurman - $50
Shania Twain - $50
Liv Tyler - $50
James Van Der Beek - $40
Michelle Williams - $45
Kate Winslet - $50

Jennifer Love Hewitt - $50
Sarah Michelle Gellar - $50
Britney Spears - $50

ORIGINAL 27"x40" ONE-SHEET MOVIE POSTERS

American Beauty - $16
Any Given Sunday - $16
Anywhere But Here - $16
Austin Powers 2 - $18
Blair Witch Project - $25
Bone Collector - $16
Bringing Out the Dead - $16
Dogma - $18
Double Jeopardy - $16
Drive Me Crazy - $16
End of Days - $16
Fight Club - $16
For Love of the Game - $16
Green Mile - $18
Hanging Up - $16
I Know What You Did Last Summer - $18
Insider - $16
Man on the Moon - $16
Matrix - $25

Mummy - $16
Pokemon: First Movie - $18
Saving Private Ryan - $25
Scream - $25
Scream 3 - $18
Shakespeare in Love - $16
Sixth Sense - $16
Sleepy Hollow - $18
Star Wars Episode 1 - Call
Stigmata - $16
Story of Us - $16
Talented Mr. Ripley - $16
Teaching Mrs. Tingle - $16
Three Kings - $16
Three to Tango - $16
Titanic - $25
Wild Things - $16
World is Not Enough - $16
X-Files Movie - $25

Attention retailers: authorized dealers receive 25% off. Please call for information.

Sports & Entertainment Memorabilia
AUTOGRAPHS ✰ MOVIE & MUSIC POSTERS ✰ PHOTOS
LIMITED EDITIONS ✰ TOYS ✰ AMERICANA & MORE !!

Call for a free catalog or visit our website to view & order over 10,000 products on-line at WWW.UNIQUECOLLECTIBLES.COM

FOR ORDERS, INFORMATION OR A FREE COLOR CATALOG
CALL TOLL FREE 1-888-725-7614

Mail Orders: Truly Unique Collectibles, MV-01, P.O. Box 29, Suffern, NY 10901.
Please include $5.95 shipping for U.S. orders & $10.95 for International.

Truly Unique Collectibles
MOVIES • TV • MUSIC • SCI-FI • SPORTS • MODELS

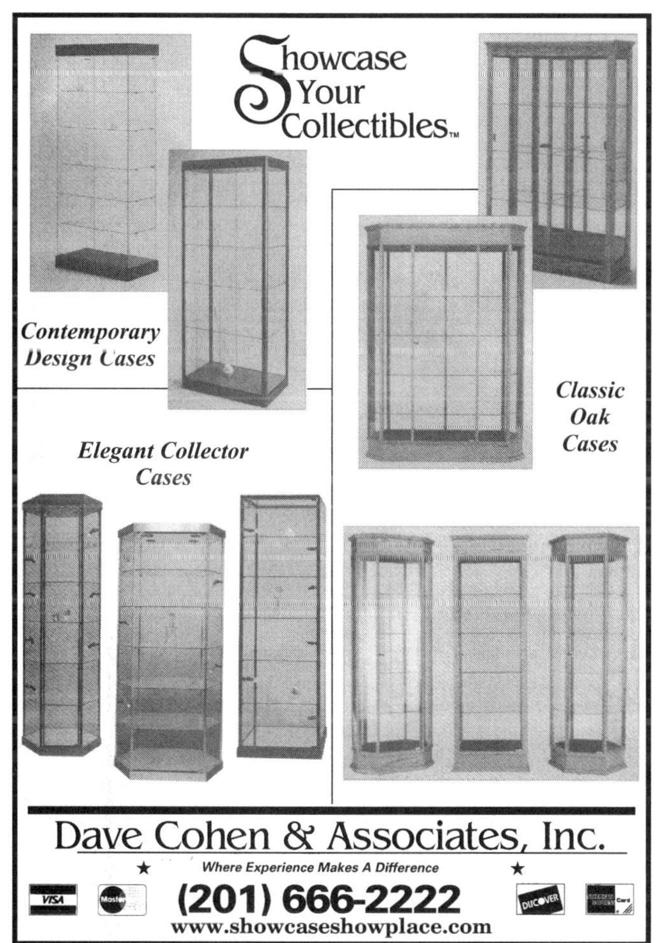

Showcase Your Collectibles™
Contemporary Design Cases
Elegant Collector Cases
Classic Oak Cases
Dave Cohen & Associates, Inc.
Where Experience Makes A Difference
(201) 666-2222
www.showcaseshowplace.com
VISA   MasterCard   DISCOVER

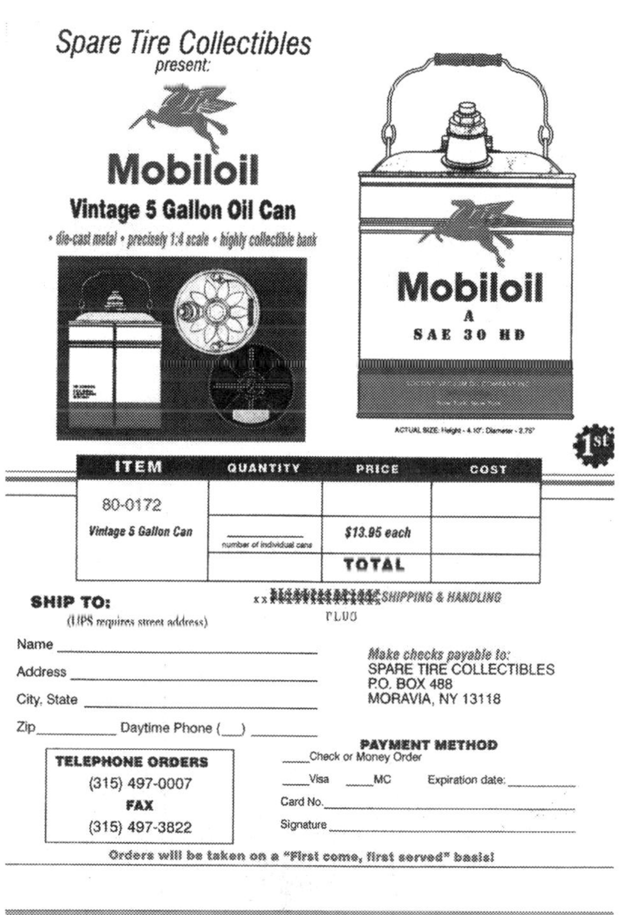

Spare Tire Collectibles present:
Mobiloil
Vintage 5 Gallon Oil Can
• die-cast metal • precisely 1:4 scale • highly collectible bank
Mobiloil
A
SAE 30 HD
ACTUAL SIZE: Height - 4.10"; Diameter - 2.75"
1st

ITEM   QUANTITY   PRICE   COST
80-0172
Vintage 5 Gallon Can   number of individual cans $13.95 each
TOTAL

SHIP TO:
(UPS requires street address)
Name
Address
City, State
Zip   Daytime Phone (   )

xxx RECOMMENDED SHIPPING & HANDLING
PLUS

Make checks payable to:
SPARE TIRE COLLECTIBLES
P.O. BOX 488
MORAVIA, NY 13118

PAYMENT METHOD
____Check or Money Order
____Visa   ____MC   Expiration date:
Card No.
Signature

TELEPHONE ORDERS
(315) 497-0007
FAX
(315) 497-3822

Orders will be taken on a "First come, first served" basis!

Toy Shop Is Open!

Come on in! **Toy Shop** opens endless possibilities for great buys and fair deals for *buyers and sellers, collectors and dealers.* Browse with thousands from coast to coast! **Plus,** you get great news articles that will fill you in on the latest in the world of toys.

SUBSCRIBE NOW!

★ **THOUSANDS OF ADS - CLASSIFIED AND DISPLAY**
★ **AUCTIONS ★ SHOWS ★ TRAVELERS DIRECTORY**
★ **MUCH, MUCH MORE**

Save $5.00!

Mail with payment to:
Toy Shop
Dept. ABAW88
700 E. State St., Iola, WI, 54990-0001

❑ **YES!** Sign me up for 26 issues (1 year) of **Toy Shop** for only **$28.95**
❑ Payment enclosed ❑ MasterCard ❑ VISA ❑ Discover/Novus ❑ American Express

Name ___________________________
Address ___________________________
City ___________________ State _________ Zip ___________
Phone ___________________________
Card No. ___________________________
Expires: Mo. _______________ Yr. _______________
Signature ___________________________

SAVE $74.50 OFF THE SINGLE COPY PRICE!

Credit Card Orders Are Toll-Free!

800-258-0929

Monday-Friday, 7 a.m. - 8 p.m.
Saturday 8 a.m. - 2 p.m.; CST

Dept. ABAW88

Visit our web site: www.toyshopmag.com

Offer good in U.S.A. Write for foreign rates.

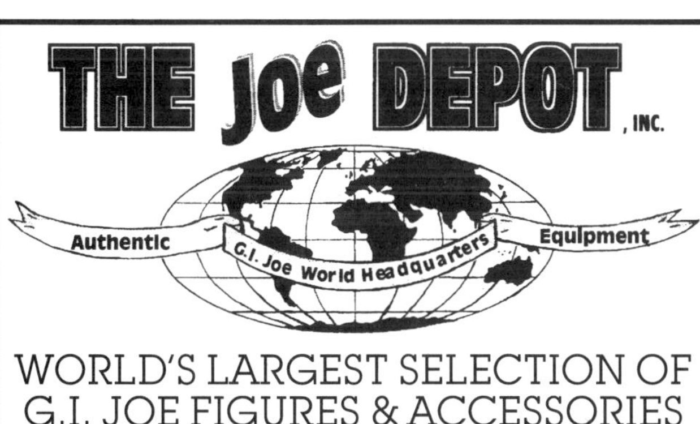

WORLD'S LARGEST SELECTION OF G.I. JOE FIGURES & ACCESSORIES

Phone or FAX (215) 721-9749
P.O. Box 228, Kulpsville, PA 19443-0228

http:www.ewtech.com/gijoe/

ALWAYS BUYING G.I. JOE COLLECTIONS
Now Accepting:

Visit Akron-Canton's Largest Selection of Classic Toys & TV Memorabilia at:

The Toys Time Forgot

"Originality Can Never Be Duplicated"

SPECIALIZING IN RECAPTURING YOUR CHILDHOOD MEMORIES FOR 10 YEARS

Step into the past with 1400 sq. ft. of memories and blasts from the past with our toys and TV memorabilia

- 20 years collecting experience
- FREE Comic Membership
- Comic Books Old & New
- Disney Collectabales
- Non Sports Cards ('40 - Present)
- Tin Wind-ups & Battery Ops
- Action Figures

- FREE Appraisals
- Star Wars - Star Trek
- Superhero Toys
- TV Board Games
- Barbies - G.I. Joes
- Hot Wheels - Matchbox
- Robots - Transformers

We Specialize in "Baby Boomer" vintage toys.

We Buy Toy Collections Big and Small!!!

Dan Hare, 102 S. Canal St., Canal Fulton, OH 44614

888-TTT-4GOT • (330) 854-1700 • FAX (330) 854-6902

Toy Dealer Directory

Note: When two numbers are listed, the first is a phone number; the second is a fax number.

Action Figures

MJR Needful Thingz
530 Savage Ct.
Longwood, FL 32750
800-841-7610 / 407-261-0134

Rebel Toy
2300 California St.
Placentia, CA 92870
714-579-0673 / 714-579-0673

Village Comics
214 Sullivan St.
New York, NY 10012
212-777-2770 / 212-475-9727

New Force Comics and Collectibles
5834 SW 146th Ct.
Miami, FL 33183
305-387-0760 / 305-387-9040

M & J Variety
932 East Boulevard
Alpha, NJ 08865
908-213-9099 / 908-213-1599

Just Be Distribution
111 N.W. 2nd Ave.
Portland, OR 97209
503-796-2733 / 503-796-3863

Brian's Toys
W730 Hwy. 35, P.O. Box 95
Fountain City, WI 54629
608-687-7572 / 608-687-7573

Small Blue Planet Toys
800-320-0890

MJR Needful Thingz

carries a full line of Action Figures including KISS, Lady Death, Puppet Master, Star Trek, Star Wars, Warrior Nun Areala, and Witchblade.

Vist us on the internet at
http://www.mjrneedfulthingz.com

530 Savage Court • Longwood, FL 32750
Phone: 407-261-0133 or 800-841-7610
Fax: 407-261-0134

Mike Lombard
4009-B Nebraska Ave.
Nashville, TN 37209
615-297-1360 / 615-292-2219

Old Forest Press
223 Wall St.
Huntington, NY 11743

Tally Ho Studios
639 Park Ave., S.W.
Canton, OH 44706
330-452-4488

Creepy
3770 Vinton Ave., #3
Los Angeles, CA 90034
310-836-3130

Toys Time Forgot
102 S. Canal St.
Canal Fulton, OH 44614
330-854-1700 / 330-854-6902

Airplanes for Sale

Apple Patch Toys
RR1 Box 338
Branchville, NJ 07826

ARCH, Inc.

1:48 Scale Die-cast replicas
Makers of the only authentic authorized T-34 Mentor
Also offering 1929 Biplane
Coming in 2000 - the AT6/SNJ
Dealers invited   Custom Imprint Available
7 Hyatt Road, P.O. Box 458
Branchville, NJ 07826
Phone 973-702-0440, Fax 973-702-1699
E-mail: molly@archtheworld.com
www.archtheworld.com

APPLE PATCH TOYS, INC.

DIE-CAST AIRPLANES BY:
ARCH, Inc. ARMOUR, CORGI, SpecCast, Ertl
SERVING COLLECTORS SINCE 1989
7 Hyatt Road, Branchville, NJ 07826
Phone 973-702-0008, Fax 973-702-1699
e-mail: sales@applepatchtoys.com
www.applepatchtoys.com
FREE BROCHURE
Shop online at BuyByByte.com

Arch Inc.
P.O. Box 458
Branchville, NJ 07826

Crazyladycollectibles
28 Edgemoor Rd.
Timonium, MD 21093
410-252-0379

Wings and Wheel
66 Whittier Rd.
Medford, MA 02155
781-396-6266 / 781-396-5617

Airplanes Wanted

Dan Wells Antique Toys
P.O. Box 7
Goshen, KY 40026
502-292-1748 / 502-292-1749

Announcements/Shows

Remember When Antique and Flea Market
6240 Chambersburg Rd.
Fayetteville, PA 17222
717-352-4762

Vaughn Crispin
524 Weldon St.
Latrobe, PA 15650
724-537-5574 / 724-537-5584

Brimfield Associates
P.O. Box 1800
Ocean City, NJ 08226
609-926-1800

Wayne Gately Productions

P.O. Box 221052
Sacramento, CA 95822
916-448-2655

Buffalo Toy Show and Auction
25 Tiernon Park
Buffalo, NY 14223
716-837-4023

Old Country Barn
1554 Holly Pike
Carlisle, PA 17013
717-245-9303

Brokaw's
P.O. Box 360033
Decatur, GA 30036
770-987-2773

Antique Toys for Sale

Gasoline Alley
6501 20th Ave. NE
Seattle, WA 98115
206-524-1606

Toys Time Forgot
102 S. Canal St.
Canal Fulton, OH 44614
330-854-1700 / 330-854-6902

Steven Agin
P.O. Box 68
Delaware, NJ 07833
908 475 1796

Auctions

Hake's Americana & Collectibles
P.O. Box 1444
York, PA 17405
717-848-1333 / 717-852-0344

International Toy Collectors
Association (ITCA)
RR2 Box 90V
Athens, IL 62613
217-351-9437 / 217-351-9437

Cars for Sale

Budget Minder Collectibles
701 E. Bay St. #1017
Charleston, SC 29403
843-577-7695 / 843-577-9494

Yankee Peddler
Box 205
Lothian, MD 20711
410-741-9080 / 410-741-9123

Peter St. Yves
3 Fieldstone Dr.
Lakeville, MA 02347
508-947-3911

Michael Silver
509 Danielle Ct.
Roseville, CA 95747
916-782-4800 / 916-782-4802

Thortek
2800-A West Main
League City, TX 77573
800-829-1520 / 281-557-1426

Jeff's Collectibles & Sportswear
2318 South 72nd St.
Lincoln, NE 68506
402-489-1800 / 402-489-1799

Catalogs, Collectible

Tom's Sci-Fi Shop
P.O. Box 56116
Harwood Heights, IL 60706-0116

Character Toys for Sale

Dolores Bauder
81 Sugarberry Rd.
Clinton, SC 29325
864 833 2481

CRM 2000
P.O. Box 631163
Houston, TX 77263
713-785-1566

Tatonka Toys & Collectibles
1234 Harbor Cove
Woodstock, GA 30189
770-516-6874 / 770-516-5791

Steve and Cathy Sawchuk
2590 Allen Crescent
Brossard, Quebec, Canada J4Z 3C2
450-676-6424 / 450-676-3256

M & J Variety
932 East Boulevard
Alpha, NJ 08865
908-213-9099 / 908 213 1599

Budget Minder Collectibles
701 E. Bay St. #1017
Charleston, SC 29403
843-577-7695 / 843-577-9494

MJR Needful Thingz
530 Savage Ct.
Longwood, FL 32750
800-841-7610 / 407-261-0134

Brian's Toys
W730 Hwy. 35, P.O. Box 95
Fountain City, WI 54629
608-687-7572 / 608-687-7573

Toys Time Forgot
102 S. Canal St.
Canal Fulton, OH 44614
330-854-1700 / 330-854-6902

Okutani Corporation
1320 Landmeier Rd.
Elk Grove Village, IL 60007
847-437-0009 / 847-437-0090

Character Toys Wanted

Ghoulie Motors
674 Portland St.
Rochester, NH 03867
603-335-0555 / 603-335-8683

Decades
110 West 4th St.
Royal Oak, MI 48067
248-546-9289 / 248-546-5803

Gary Hein
P.O. Box 179
Little Silver, NJ 07739
732-224-8760 / 732-219-5940

Yankee Peddler
Box 205
Lothian, MD 20711
410-741-9080 / 410-741-9123

The Doll & Hobby Shoppe
138 S. Woodland Blvd
Deland, FL 32720
990-734-3200

Logan's Claw Toys
5415 Sepulveda Blvd.
Culver City, CA 90230
888-456-4505

Thortek
2800-A West Main
League City, TX 77573
800-829-1520 / 281-557-1426

Matchbox

The Doll & Hobby Shoppe
138 S. Woodland Blvd
Deland, FL 32720
990-734-3200 / 904-734-1356

Bob Steinberg
P.O. Box 900166
San Diego, CA 92190
619-583-4406

Military Soldiers

John's Collectibles & Sportscards
110-3760 Moncton St.
Richmond, B.C., Canada V7E3A6
204-275-0492

Miscellaneous Non-Toys

Adkins Collectibles
422 E. Oak St.
Oak Creek, WI 53154
414-761-1020 / 414-761-1088

Barrington Square Cards
P.O. Box 310-E
West Dundee, IL 60118
847-426-2020 / 847-426-0475

Jay Sage
P.O. Box 55073
Seattle, WA 98155
206-367-8643

Showcase Express
714-842-5564

Miscellaneous Toys for Sale

Steve and Cathy Sawchuk
2590 Allen Crescent
Brossard, Quebec, Canada J4Z 3C2
450-676-6424 / 450-676-3256

California Collectables

1060 E. 11th St.
Oakland, CA 94606
510-653-1310 / 510-465-5970

Okutani Corporation
1320 Landmeier Rd.
Elk Grove Village, IL 60007
847-437-0009 / 847-437-0090

Ghoulie Motors
674 Portland St.
Rochester, NH 03867
603-335-0555 / 603-335-8683

Decades
110 West 4th St.
Royal Oak, MI 48067
248-546-9289 / 248-546-5803

M & J Variety
932 East Boulevard
Alpha, NJ 08865
908-213-9099 / 908-213-1599

Tom Lastrapes
P.O. Box 2444
Pinellas Park, FL 33780
727-545-2586

Truly Unique Collectibles
MV-12, P.O. Box 29
Suffern, NY 10901
888-725-7614

Toys Toys Toys
P.O. Box 80433
Staten Island, NY 10308
718-966-4443 / 718-605-4978

Early Adventure
445 Gallitin Rd.
Belle Vernon, PA 15012
724-379-5833 / 724-379-5966

Trader Fred's
Rt. 132 Box 65
Thetford Center, VT 05075
802-785-2845

Alen Goldberg
461 Willow Rd. E. #2
Staten Island, NY 10314
718-761-0864

Bill Brady
9013 E. Butternut Ave.
Mesa, AZ 85208
602-984-6884

Toys Time Forgot
102 S. Canal St.
Canal Fulton, OH 44614
330-854-1700 / 330-854-6902

American Memorabilia
7500 W. Lake Mead Blvd. 9-308
Las Vegas, NV 89128
800-430-0667

Tatonka Toys & Collectibles
1234 Harbor Cove
Woodstock, GA 30189
770-516-6874 / 770-516-5791

Vintage Plastic Toys
36 MacArthur Blvd.
Danvers, MA 01923
978-774-3955

Sandbox Refugees
218-652-3889

Serious Toyz
21 Sunset Trail
Croton-on-Hudson, NY 10520
914-271-4272 / 914-827-9366

Victorian Collectables
Box 1560
Mattituck, NY 11952

Bill and Anne Campbell
1221 Littlebrook Lane
Birmingham, AL 35235
205-853-8227 / 205-853-9951

Frederick Ross
2128 N. 38th St.
Milwaukee, WI 53208
414-444-5836

Yankee Peddler
Box 205
Lothian, MD 20711
410-741-9080
410-741-9123

The Olde Toy Brigade
P.O. Box 1347
Brookhaven, PA 19015
610-876-3064 / 610-876-3064

MNM Collectibles
120 Covington Dr.
Warwick, RI 02886-1936
401-738-2277

Miscellaneous Toys Wanted

Margot and Pat Schnarr
450 Erb St. W., Suite 141
Waterloo, Ontario, Canada N2T 1H4
416-425-3966

Model Kits

Shadowland
1637 Hanover Ave.
Allentown, PA 18103
610-437-0189

Michael Silver
509 Danielle Ct.
Roseville, CA 95747
916-782-4800 / 916-782-4802

Art 'N' Things
133-S. Anderson Ave.
Fairview, NJ 07022
201-943-2288

Movie & TV Show Toys

Brian's Toys
W730 Hwy. 35, P.O. Box 95
Fountain City, WI 54629
608-687-7572 / 608-687-7573

Decades
110 West 4th St.

Royal Oak, MI 48067
248-546-9289 / 248-546-5803

Mike Lombard
4009-B Nebraska Ave.
Nashville, TN 37209
615-297-1360 / 615-292-2219

Barrington Square Cards
P.O. Box 310-E
West Dundee, IL 60118
847-426-2020 / 847-426-0475

Team Enterprises, Inc.
15615 Jamaica Lane
Fountain Hills, AZ 85268
480-837-3444 / 480-837-3444

M & J Variety
932 East Boulevard
Alpha, NJ 08865
908-213-9099 / 908-213-1599

MJR Needful Thingz
530 Savage Ct.
Longwood, FL 32750
800-841-7610

Gotham Knights
25221 Gratiot Ave.
Roseville, MI 48066
810-778-4349

Toys Time Forgot
102 S. Canal St.
Canal Fulton, OH 44614
330-854-1700 / 330-854-6902

CRM 2000
P.O. Box 631163
Houston, TX 77263
713-785-1566

Pedal Cars

Yankee Peddler
Box 205
Lothian, MD 20711
410-741-9080 / 410-741-9123

PEZ

Margot and Pat Schnarr
450 Erb St. W., Suite 141
Waterloo, Ontario, Canada N2T 1H4
416-425-3966

MJR Needful Thingz
530 Savage Ct.
Longwood, FL 32750
800-841-7610

Play Sets

Vintage Plastic Toys
36 MacArthur Blvd.
Danvers, MA 01923
978-774-3955

Publications/Books

The Windmill Group
P.O. Box 56551
Sherman Oaks, CA 91413
800-470-5540

Old Forest Press
223 Wall St.
Huntington, NY 11743

Blystone's
2132 Delaware Ave.
Pittsburgh, PA 15218
412-371-3511 / 412-244-8028

Yesteryear Toys & Books
Box 537
Alexandria Bay, NY 13607
800-481-1353 / 800-305-5138

Railroads Wanted

Cliff Robnett
7804 N.W. 27
Bethany, OK 73008
405-787-6703

Robots

Richard Johnson
P.O. Box 27093
Prescott Valley, AZ 86312
520-775-4714 / 520-771-9445

Steve and Cathy Sawchuk
2590 Allen Crescent
Brossard, Quebec, Canada J4Z 3C2
450-676-6424 / 450-676-3256

Mark Bergin
603-924-2079 / 603-924-2022

Just Be Distribution
111 N.W. 2nd Ave.
Portland, OR 97209
503-796-2733 / 503-796-3863

Art 'N' Things
133-S. Anderson Ave.
Fairview, NJ 07022
201-943-2288

Services

Collectibles Insurance Agency
P.O. Box 1200
Westminster, MD 21158
888-837-9537 / 410-876-9233

Space Toys

MJR Needful Thingz
530 Savage Ct.
Longwood, FL 32750
800-841-7610

Tally Ho Studios
639 Park Ave., S.W.

Canton, OH 44706
330-452-4488

Brian's Toys
W730 Hwy. 35, P.O. Box 95
Fountain City, WI 54629
608-687-7572 / 608-687-7573

Star Wars and Stuff
P.O. Box 58
Decatur, TX 76234
940-433-8482 / 940-433-5444

Time and Space Toys
P.O. Box 94
Newington, VA 22122-0094
703-339-8576

Mark Bergin
603-924-2079 / 603-924-2022

Trucks for Sale

Denny's Diecast & Collectibles
18 Hope Road
Levittown, PA 19056
215-943-2708

Jeff's Collectibles & Sportswear
2318 South 72nd St.
Lincoln, NE 68506
402-489-1800

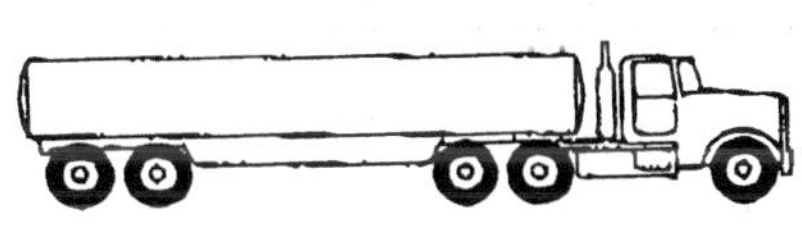

Budget Minder Collectibles
701 E. Bay St. #1017
Charleston, SC 29403
843-577-7695 / 843-577-9494

Bruce Johnson Toy Talk
702 Steeplechase Rd.
Landisville, PA 17538
717-898-2932 / 717-898-3885

Granite State Collectibles
177 Main St.
New Ipswich, NH 03071
603-878-1713 / 603-878-4509

G&K Toy Trucks
32 Stinson Pl.
Little Falls, NJ 07424
973-785-4022

B & L Toys
70 Pineview Dr.
Perfield, NY 14526
716-385-3365

Thortek
2800-A West Main
League City, TX 77573
800-829-1520 / 281-557-1426

Tom Snook
478 Sandy Way
Benicia, CA 94510
510-787-3283 / 510-787-3293

Crazyladycollectibles
28 Edgemoor Rd.
Timonium, MD 21093
410-252-0379

Vehicles, Die-Cast and Plastic

Supercar Collectibles
7311 7th Circle North
Minneapolis, MN 55428
612-425-6020

Western Toys

Brand D Auction
25836 SW Rein Rd.
Sherwood, OR 97140
503-625-5464

Wind-up & Battery Toys

Toys Time Forgot
102 S. Canal St.
Canal Fulton, OH 44614
330-854-1700 / 330-854-6902

Toy Clubs Directory

Editor's Note: This is a partial list of toy collector clubs. To have your club listed free in the next edition of the "Toy Shop Annual," send pertinent information to: Editor, "Toy Shop Annual," 700 E. State St., Iola, WI 54990.

American Game Collectors Association
Specialty: Games and puzzles
Address: P.O. Box 44, Dresher, PA 19025
Newsletter: Yes

Austin Fashion Doll Club
Specialty: Barbie dolls
Contact: Sherri Rhein
Address: 4711 Avenue F, Austin, TX 78751
Phone: 512-323-0904

Barbie and Ken Dolls Meet Wisconsin Collectors
Specialty: Barbie dolls
Contact: Katie Gorton
Address: 2545 Eastwood Ln., Brookfield, WI 53005

Barbie Club
Specialty: Barbie dolls
Contact: Tami Hall
Address: 5484 E. Swift, Fresno, CA 93727

Barbie Doll Collectors Club International
Specialty: Barbie dolls
Contact: Dora Lerch
Address: P.O. Box 586, White Plains, NY 10603
Phone: 914-362-4657

Brenda Starr Comic Strip Fan Club
Specialty: Brenda Starr collectibles
Contact: R. Robert Pollak
Address: 56 Livingston St., Brooklyn, NY 11201

Cabbage Patch Kids Collectors' Club
Specialty: Cabbage Patch Kids dolls
Address: P.O. Box 714, Cleveland, GA 30528
Phone: 706-865-2171

Chair City Barbie Club
Specialty: Barbie dolls
Address: P.O. Box 3072, Thomasville, NC 27361
Phone: 336-475-7110

Cracker Jack Collectors Association
Specialty: Cracker Jack and related memorabilia
Contact: Ron Toth
Address: 72 Charles St., Rochester, NH 03867-3413
Phone: 603-335-2062
Newsletter: Monthly

G.I. Joe Collectors' Club Chicago Area Division
Specialty: G.I. Joe and other 12-inch and 3-3/4-inch figures
Contact: Kevin Bolger
Address: 510 N. Prospect Manor Ave., Mount Prospect, IL 60056
Phone: 847-577-8437
Annual Dues: $10
Newsletter: Five times per year

Johnny Lightning News Flash
Specialty: Johnny Lightning die-cast cars
Contact: Playing Mantis Toys
Address: 3600 McGill St., Suite 300, P.O. Box 3688, South Bend, IN 46619
Phone: 219-232-0300
Newsletter: Yes

Larry's Traders
Specialty: Trading Cards
Contact: Larry Jackson
Address: 509 Ashland, Aurora, IL 60505

Phone: 630-851-9074
Annual Dues: $6

Looky's
Specialty: Hot Wheels
Contact: Omar
Address: 1603 N. Thurmond St., Winston-Salem, NC 27105

Lords of Darkness
Specialty: Fantasy, JRR Tolkien, Lord of the Rings
Contact: Paul Clement
Address: 11 Morningside Dr., Latham, NY 12110
Phone: 518-785-5099
Annual Dues: $20

M & M Collectors Club
Specialty: Promotional Items
Contact: Nancy Pinto
Address: 120 Covington Dr., Warwick, RI 02886-1936
Phone: 401-738-2277
Newsletter: M & M Happenings

Madison Area Die-Cast Collectors Club
Specialty: Die-Cast Vehicles
Contact: Terry F. Nadosy
Address: P.O. Box 817, Spring Green, WI 53588
Phone: 608-588-3133
Annual Dues: $12
Newsletter: Monthly

Marble Collector's Society of America
Specialty: Marbles
Address: P.O. Box 222, Trumbull, CT 06611
Newsletter: Quarterly

Matchbox Collectors Guild
Specialty: Matchbox Collectibles
Address: P.O. Box 10490, Glendale, AZ 85318-0490
Phone: 800-858-0102

**Matchbox Premiere
Collectors Club**
Specialty: Matchbox die-cast cars
Address: P.O. Box 804,
  Conshohocken, PA 19428
Phone: 800-524-8697
Newsletter: Yes

Mazda Collectors Club
Specialty: Mazda die-cast, kits, etc.
Contact: Werner Legrand
Address: Postbus 5, Brecht,
  Belgium B2960
Phone: 323-373-4498
Newsletter: Bi-annual

**McDonald's Collectors Club,
  Florida Sunshine Chapter**
Specialty: McDonald's Fast Food
  Toys
Contact: Bill and Pat Poe
Address: 2220 Dominica Circle E.,
  Niceville, FL 32578-4085
Phone: 850-897-4163
Annual Dues: $15
Newsletter: monthly

Motor City Hot Wheels
Specialty: Hot Wheels
Contact: Steve Cinnamon
Address: P.O. Box 55, Belleville,
  MI 48112-0055
Phone: 313-699-2170

**Nebraska, the Good Life
  with Barbie**
Specialty: Barbie dolls
Contact: Laree Skeleton
Address: 735 Nye St., Fremont, NE
  68025
Phone: 402-727-6148

Pacific NW Doll Collectors Club
Specialty: Barbies, Beanies, Gene
  Dolls
Contact: Kathy Anderberg
Address: 4701 225th Pl. SW,
  Mountlake Terrace, WA 98043
Phone: 425-778-2442
Annual Dues: $10
Newsletter: Monthly

PVC Collectors Club
Specialty: Cartoon and Character
  Figures
Contact: Colleen Lewis

Address: 10120 Main St., Clarence,
  NY 14031
Phone: 716-759-7451
Newsletter: Quarterly

**Smurf Collectors' Club
  International**
Specialty: Smurfs
Contact: Suzann Lipschitz
Address: 24T9A Cabot Rd. W.,
  Massapequa, NY 11758
Phone: 516-799-3221
Newsletter: Quarterly

**Star Wars Collectors Club of
  Southern California**
Specialty: Star Wars
Contact: David W. Carr
Address: 20201 Burnt Tree lane,
  Walnut, CA 91789-1806
Phone: 909-594-1151
Annual Dues: $5
Newsletter: Yes

**Still Bank Collectors Club
  of America**
Specialty: Still banks
Contact: Larry Egelhoff
Address: 4175 Millersville Rd.,
  Indianapolis, IN 46205
Phone: 317-846-7228

Suds City Hot Wheels Club
Specialty: Hot Wheels
Contact: Tim Pryal
Address: 7129 W. Moltke #3,
  Milwaukee, WI 53210
Phone: 414-447-6854
Newsletter: Suds City News

The Garfield Collector
Specialty: Garfield and Related
  Characters
Contact: Adrienne Warren
Address: 1032 Feather Bed Lane,
  Edison, NJ 08800-1237
Phone: 732-381-7083
Annual Dues: 5
Newsletter: No

Toy Car Collectors Club
Specialty: Toy Vehicles
Contact: Peter Foss
Address: 33290 West 14 Mile Rd.
  #454, West Bloomfield, MI
  48322

Phone: 248-682-0272

Tucson Miniature Auto Club
Specialty: Vehicle Toys
Contact: Lou Pariseau
Address: 1111 E. Limberlost Dr.
  #164, Tucson, AZ 85719-1062
Phone: 520-293-3178
Annual Dues: $10
Newsletter: Monthly

Wheels are Spinning
Specialty: Hot Wheels
Contact: Dan Hammond II
Address: 207 Kimberly Way,
  Winchester, VA 22601-5579
Phone: 540-667-2430
Annual Dues: $15
Newsletter: Monthly

**Wheels of Fire Hot Wheels Club
  of Arizona**
Specialty: Hot Wheels
Contact: Valerie Griffin
Address: P.O. Box 86431, Phoenix,
  AZ 85080
Phone: 602-848-1521
Annual Dues: $20
Newsletter: Monthly

**Williams Grove Historical Steam
  Engine Association**
Specialty: Antique Steam Engines
  and Tractors
Contact: Show Secretary
Address: Box 509, Mechanicsburg,
  PA 17055
Phone: 717-766-4001
Annual Dues: $5
Newsletter: Yes

**Windy City Collector's
  Barbie Doll Club**
Specialty: Barbie dolls
Address: P.O. Box 417518,
  Chicago, IL 60641

**Williams Grove Historical Steam
  Engine Association**
Specialty: Antique steam engines
  and tractors
Address: P.O. Box 509,
  Mechanicsburg, PA 17055
Phone: 717-766-4001
Annual Dues: $5
Newsletter: Yes

Manufacturers Directory

Have you ever wanted to reach a toy manufacturer but didn't know how? This list can help.

While not all-inclusive, this list includes many notable toy and toy-related companies currently in business. Remember, many companies will not comment on the secondary market values of their toys. Comments and questions should generally be directed to the customer service department.

21st Century Toys
Action figures
2037 Clement Ave.
Alameda, CA 94501-1317
510-814-0719
www.21stcenturytoys.com

Action Performance
Die-cast cars
4707 E. Baseline Rd.
Phoenix, AZ 85040
602-337-3824
www.action-performance.com

Aladdin Industries
Lunch kits
703 Murfreesboro Rd.
Nashville, TN 37210
800-456-1233

Alexander Doll Company
Dolls
615 W. 131st St.
New York, NY 10027-7982
212-283-5900
www.alexanderdoll.com

ALPI International
Squeezies, miscellaneous toys
1186 63rd St.
Oakland, CA 94608
510-655-6456

Applause
Plush, PVC figures
merged with Dakin in 1995
6101 Variel Ave.
Woodland Hills, CA 91365-4183
818-992-6000

Bachmann Industries
Toy trains, planes
1400 E. Erie Ave.
Philadelphia, PA 19124
215-533-1600

Bandai America
Action figures
5551 Katella Ave.
Cypress, CA 90630
714-816-9500
www.bandai.com

Basic Fun
Key chains
1080 Industrial Hwy.
Southampton, PA 18966
800-662-3380
www.basicfun.com

Bburago
Die-cast vehicles
P.O. Box 221220
Hollywood, FL 33022
800-344-4406

Berk Co.
Foam toys, games, others
bought by JAKKS Pacific in 1999
2850 E. Cedar St., Suite B
Ontario, CA 91761
909-923-0255

Binney & Smith
Crayola products, Silly Putty
P.O. Box 431, 1100 Church Lane
Easton, PA 19042
610-253-6271
www.crayola.com

Brio Corp.
Developmental toys, others
N120 W18485 Freistadt Road
Germantown, WI 53022
414-250-3240

Buffalo Games
Games
220 James E. Casey Drive
Buffalo, NY 14206
716-827-8393

Bullyland
Prehistoric replicas, others
65W 55 Street 4 Floor
New York, NY 10019
212-974-9815

Cadaco
Games
founded 1935, previously known as Cadaco-Ellis
4300 W. 47th St.
Chicago, IL 60632-4477
312-927-1500
www.cadaco.com

Cardinal Industries
Games
21-01 51st Ave.
Long Island City, NY 11101
718-784-3000

Classic Metal Works
Die-cast vehicles
6465 Monroe St.
Suite 204
Sylvania, OH 43560
419-885-1448

Code 3 Collectibles
Die-cast vehicles
6115 Variel Ave.
Woodland Hills, CA 91367
818-598-2298
www.code3.net

Corgi
See Zindart

Craft House Corporation
Lindberg model kits
328 N. Westwood Ave.
Toledo, OH 43607-3343
419-536-8351

Danbury Mint
Die-cast vehicles
47 Richards Ave.
Norwalk, CT 06857-0001
203-853-2000

Darda, Inc.
Vehicle toys, etc.
1600 Union Ave.
Baltimore, MD 21211-1917
410-889-1023

Duncan Toys
Yo-yos
15981 Valplast Rd.
Middlefield, OH 44062
216-632-1631
www.yo-yo.com

Eastwood Automobilia
Die-cast vehicles, banks
distributor of die-cast vehicles,
banks
Box 3014, Dept. PR
Malvern, PA 19355-0714
800-343-9353

Effanbee Doll Co.
Dolls
19 Lexington Ave.
East Brunswick, NY 08816
732-613-3852

Empire
Pre-school vehicles, others
acquired Buddy L in 1995
5150 Linton Blvd.
Delray Beach, FL 33484
561-498-4000

Endless Games
Games
22 Hudson Place, Room 1
Hoboken, NJ 07030
201-386-9465
www.endlessgames.com

Exoto
Die-cast vehicles
5440 Atlantis Court
Moor Park, CA 93021
805-530-3830

Figures Toy Company
Action figures
15 Puritan Ave.
Cranston, RI 02920
401-946-5720
www.figurestoycompany.com

First Gear
Die-cast models
P.O. Box 52
Peosta, IA 52068-0052
319-582-2071

Fisher-Price
Plastic preschool toys, vintage
wood pull toys
1930-present; division of Mattel
636 Girard Ave.
East Aurora, NY 14052
716-687-3449

Flatt World Figures
Action figures
P.O. Box 51790
Livonia, MI 48151
888-66-FLATT
www.flattworld.com

Flexible Flyer
Sleds
100 Tubb Ave., P.O. Box 1296
West Point, MS 39773
601-494-4732

Franklin Mint
Die-cast vehicles
Franklin Center, PA 19091-0001
800-523-7622

Full Moon Toys
Action figures
1645 N. Vine St., 9th Floor
Los Angeles, CA 90028
213-468-0599
www.fullmoontoys.com

Fun 4 All
Key chains, miscellaneous
156 Fifth Ave., Suite 823
New York, NY 10010
212-727-8833

G Whiz Enterprises
Lunch box repros
formerly Wonder Planet
14732 Lull St.
Van Nuys, CA 91405
626-683-9200

Galoob Toys
Action figures, Micro-Machines
bought by Hasbro in 1998
500 Forbes Blvd. S.
San Francisco, CA 94080
415-873-0680
www.galoob.com

Gearbox Toys & Collectibles
Die-cast vehicles
4515 20th Ave. S.W.
Cedar Rapids, IA 52404
319-390-1405

GEOmetric Design
Vinyl, resin model kits
122 S. Wabasha St.
Suite 340
St. Paul, MN 55107
612-291-1909
www.geometricdesign.com

Gordy International
Miscellaneous
P.O. Box 2769
900 North Ave.
Plainfield, NJ 07062
908-755-9660

Graphitti Designs
Action figures
1140 N. Kraemer Blvd., Unit B
Anaheim, CA 92806-1919
800-699-0115
www.graphittidesigns.com

Gund
Plush
1898-present
1 Runyons Lane, P.O. Box H
Edison, NJ 08818
908-248-1500
www.gund.com

Hallmark
Kiddie Car Classics die-cast
models
2525 Gillham Rd.
Kansas City, MO 64108-2622
816-274-8519

**Hartland Plastics/Steven Manu-
facturing**
Western/sports figures
224 E. Fourth St.
Hermann, MO 65041
314-486-5494

Hasbro Toy Group
Miscellaneous
*1940s present; previously known as
Hassenfeld Bros.; includes Kenner,
Milton Bradley, Parker Brothers,
Tonka, Playskool, Galoob*
1027 Newport Ave.
Pawtucket, RI 02862-1059
401-727-5582
www.hasbrocollectors.com

Idea Factory
Plush
1350 Broadway, Ste. 2400
New York, NY 10018
212-564-7430

Irwin
Road race sets, games, others
2200 Corporate Blvd.
Suite 306
Boca Raton, FL 33431
561-988-0870
www.irwin-toy.com

JAKKS Pacific
Wrestling action figures, others
22761 Pacific Coast Highway,
Suite 226
Malibu, CA 90265
310-456-7799
www.jakkspacific.com

Just Toys
Miscellaneous
50 W. 23rd St., 7th Floor
New York, NY 10010-5205
212-645-6335

Kenner Products
Action figures, G.I. Joe
Hasbro dropped name in 1999
615 Elsinore Pl.
Cincinnati, OH 45202
513-579-4927
www.hasbrocollectors.com

Kid Galaxy
Dolls, others
One Sundial Ave., Ste. 310
Manchester, NH 03103
603-645-6252
www.kidgalaxy.com

Krause Publications
Hobby magazines, books (*Toy Shop,* etc.)
1952-present
700 E. State St.
Iola, WI 54990
715-445-2214
www.krause.com
www.collectit.net

Larami Corp.
Miscellaneous
303 Fellowship Road, Suite 110

Mount Laurel, NJ 08054
609-439-1717

Legends In 3 Dimensions
2032 Armacost Ave.
Los Angeles, CA 90025
310-442-0156

LEGO Systems
Construction toys
555 Taylor Rd., P.O. Box 1600
Enfield, CT 06083-1600
203-763-6731
www.lego.com

Lionel Trains
Electric trains
1900-present
50625 Richard W. Blvd.
Chesterfield, MI 48051
810-949-4100
www.lionel.com

Little Tikes
Preschool toys
division of Rubbermaid
2180 Barlow Rd.
Hudson, OH 44236
216-650-3000
www.rubbermaid.com

Living Toys
Krofft superstars toys
6320 Canoga Ave., Suite 1550
Woodland Hills, CA 91367
818-227-5014

Maisto International
Die-cast vehicles
7751 Cherry Ave.
Fontana, CA 92336
909-357-7988

Majorette Toys/Solido
Die-cast vehicles
2898NW 79th Ave.
Miami, FL 33122
305-593-6016

Marklin
Toy trains
distributor of German trains
16988 W. Victor Rd.,
New Berlin, WI 53151-0319
414-784-1095

Marx Toy Company
Miscellaneous
modern reincarnation of famed Louis Marx toy Company
249 E. Sebring Ave.
Sebring, OH 44672
330-938-8697

Matchbox Collectibles
Die-cast Vehicles
6000 Midlantic Dr.
Mount Laurel, NJ 08054
609-840-1511

Mattel Toys
Barbie, Hot Wheels
1945-present; acquired Tyco in 1997; acquired Pleasant Company in 1998
333 Continental Blvd.
El Segundo, CA 90245-5012
310-252-2000
www.mattel.com

McFarlane Toys
Spawn, other action figures
15155 Fogg St.
Plymouth, MI 48170
313-414-3500
www.spawn.com

Milton Bradley
Games
1860-present; division of Hasbro
443 Shaker Rd. E
Longmeadow, MA 01028-3149
413-525-6411

Minichamps USA
Die-cast vehicles
bought by Action Performance in 1998
14260 SW 136 St. Bldg. #7
Miami, FL 33186

Moore Action Collectibles
Action figures
3038 SE Loop 820
Fort Worth, TX 76140
817-568-2620
www.mooreaction.com

Nintendo of America
Video games
4820 150th Ave. NE

Redmond, WA 98052-5111
206-882-2040
www.nintendo.com

Nylint
Vehicle toys
1946-present
1800 Sixteenth Ave.
Rockford, IL 61104-5491
815-397-2880

OddzOn Products
Miscellaneous
purchased by Hasbro in 1997
50 Technology Court
Napa, CA 94558
707-251-3700

Ohio Art
Etch-a-Sketch, vintage tin toys
One Toy St.
Bryan, OH 43506
419-636-3141

Pac West
Mr. Octobears (plush)
7040 Avenida Encinas,
Suite 104-247
Carlsbad, CA 92009

Parker Brothers
Games
1880s-present; division of Hasbro
50 Dunham Rd.
Beverly, MA 01915
617-927-7600

Peaceable Planet
Plush
P.O. Box 23325
Savannah, GA 31403
912-651-8003
www.peaceableplanet.com

PEZ Candy
Candy dispensers
founded in 1927 in Austria
35 Prindle Hill Rd.
Orange, CT 06477
203-795-0531

Planet Plush
Plush
22 St. Joseph St.
Toronto, Canada M4Y 1J9

416-513-9464
www.planetplush.com

Playing Mantis
Johnny Lightning die-cast, model kits, action figures
3600 McGill St., 3300, P.O. Box 3688
South Bend, IN 46619-3688
219-232-0300
www.playingmantis.com

Playmates Toys
Action figures
611 Anton Blvd. #600
Costa Mesa, CA 92626
714-428-2000
www.playmatestoys.com

Playmobil USA
Figures, play sets
22-E Nichols Ct.
Dayton, NJ 08810
908-274-0101
www.playmobil.com

Playskool
Preschool toys
division of Hasbro
1027 Newport Ave.
Pawtucket, RI 02862-1059

Poof Toy Products
Foam toys
bought James Industries (Slinky) in 1998
45400 Helm St.
Plymouth, MI 48170
313-454-9552

Pressman Toy
Games
1920s-present
200 Fifth Ave., Suite 1052
New York, NY 10010
212-675-7910

Racing Champions/Ertl
Die-cast vehicles, farm toys, banks
1945-present
purchased Ertl in 1999
Highways 136 & 20, P.O. Box 500
Dyersville, IA 52040-0500
319-875-5607
www.racingchamps.com

Radio Flyer
Wagons
6515 West Grand Ave.
Chicago, IL 60635
800-621-7613
www.radioflyer.com

Reeves International
Distributor of Breyer horses
14 Industrial Rd.
Pequannock, NJ 07440
201-694-5006

Rendition Figures
Action figures
16519 Wildnerness Rd.
Poway, CA 92064
619-592-6866

Resaurus
Action figures
240 Outerbelt St.
Columbus, OH 43213
614-751-9352
www.resaurus.com

Revell-Monogram
Model kits
8601 Waukegan Rd.
Morton Grove, IL 60053
708-966-3500
www.revell-monogram.com

Road Champs
Vehicle toys
division of JAKKS Pacific
7 Patton Dr.
West Caldwell, NJ 07006-6404
201-228-6900

Russ Berrie & Co.
Plush
111 Bauer Dr.
Oakland, NJ 07436
201-337-9000

Sanrio, Inc.
Hello Kitty, others
570 Eccles Ave.
So. San Francisco, CA 94080
650-925-2880

Schuco/Lilliput Motor Co.
Vehicles, tin
P.O. Box 447

Yerington, NV 89447
702-463-5181

Sega of America
Video games
255 Shoreline Dr.
Redwood City, CA 94065
415-508-2800
www.sega.com

Shadowbox Collectibles
Specialty figures
1578 N.W. 165th St.
Miami, FL 33169
305-621-0545
www.shadowboxinc.com

Sideshow
Action figures, others
31364 Via Colinas, Suite 106
Westlake Village, CA 91362
818-879-1996

Smith-Miller
Vehicle toys
P.O. Box 139
Canoga Park, CA 91305
818-703-8588

SpecCast
Die-cast vehicles
428 6th Ave. NW
Dyersville, IA 52040-1129
319-875-8706

Steiff USA
Plush, teddy bears
founded in 1880 in Germany
200 Fifth Ave., Suite 1205
New York, NY 10010
212-675-2727

Tamiya America
Miscellaneous
2 Orion
Aliso Viejo, CA 92656-4200
714-362-2240
www.tamiya.com

Thinkway Toys
Disney products, electronic banks,
miscellaneous
8885 Woodbine Ave.
Markham, Ontario Canada
L3R 5G9

905-470-8883
www.thinkwaytoys.com

Tiger Electronics
Electronic games
purchased by Hasbro in 1998
980 Woodlands Parkway
Vernon Hills, IL 60061
847-913-8100

Today's Kids
Miscellaneous
formerly Wolverine
13630 Neutron Road
Dallas, TX 75244
972-404-9335

Tonka
See Hasbro

Tootsietoy / Strombecker
Vehicle toys, other
600 N. Pulaski Rd.
Chicago, IL 60624
312-638-1000

Toy Biz
Action figures
P.O. Box 90113
Allentown, PA 18109
800-634-7539

Toy Island
Miscellaneous
100 Universal Plaza Bldg. 10
Universal City, CA 91608
818-733-7500

Toy Vault
Action figures
P.O. Box 1915
London, KY 40743
606-864-8658
www.toyvault.com

Trendmasters
Action figures
611 North 10th St., Suite 555
St. Louis, MO 63101
314-231-2250

Ty, Inc.
Beanie Babies
P.O. Box 5377
Oakbrook, IL 60522

800-876-8000
www.ty.com

Tyco Industries
See Mattel

Uncle Milton Industries
Science, nature, exploration toys
5717 Corsa Ave.
Westlake Village, CA 91362
818-707-0800
www.unclemilton.com

U.S. Games Systems
Games, playing cards
179 Ludlow St.
Stamford, CT 06902
203-353-8400

USAOPOLY
565 Westlake St.
*creator and distributor of specialty
Monopoly games*
Encintias, CA 92024
888-876-7659
www.usaopoly.com

Winross
Die-cast trucks
1965-present
Box 23860
Rochester, NY 14692
716-381-5638

Wizards of the Coast
Role-Playing Games, Pokémon,
Magic: The Gathering
bought by Hasbro in 1999
P.O. Box 707
Renton, WA 98057
800-238-3114
www.wizards.com

X Toys
Action figures
27 Beach Road
Monmouth Beach, NJ 07750
732-870-1424

Zindart
U.S. distributor of Corgi
160 Sansome St., 18F
San Francisco, CA 94104
415-273-7094

2000 Toy Show Calendar

ALABAMA

Mar 11 2000 AL, Fairhope. March Fantasy Doll & Toy Show. Civic Ctr. Auditorium. SH: 9:30am-4pm, A: $2., $1. ages 6-12. Doris Perdue, PO Box 386, Montrose, AL 36559. PH: 334-928-0855.

ARIZONA

Jan 22 2000 AZ, Phoenix. Toy Round-Up. State Fairgrounds, 19th Ave. & McDowell. SH: 9am-3pm, A: $3. Jack Black Enterprises, PO Box 61172, Phoenix, AZ 85082. PH: 602-943-1766.

Feb 5 2000 AZ, Yuma. Golden Age of Dolls. Civic & Convention Ctr., 1440 Desert Hills Dr. SH: 10am-4pm. Richard Morris, PO Box 5032, Yuma, AZ 85366. PH: 520-783-1364.

Mar 12 2000 AZ, Tucson. 12th Annual TMAC Collectible Toy Show. Marketplace USA, 3750 E. Irvington Rd. SH: 9am-3pm, A: $2., under 13 free with adult. Lou Pariseau, PH: 520-293-3178.

Sep 30 2000 AZ, Mesa. 2nd Annual Toy Extravaganza. Community Ctr., Centennial Hall, 201 N. Center St. SH: 9am-4pm, T: 140, A: $2., 10 & under free. Valerie Griffin, 6977 W. San Miguel, Glendale, AZ 85303. PH: 623-848-1521.

CALIFORNIA

Jan 8-9 2000 CA, San Diego. Teddy Bear, Doll & Antique Toy Show. Scottish Rite Ctr., 1895 Camino Del Rio S. SH: Sat. 10:30am-4pm, Sun. 10am-3pm, A: $5. Linda Mullins, PO Box 2327, Carlsbad, CA 92018. PH: 760-434-7444 or FAX: 760-434-0154.

Jan 16 2000 CA, Santa Clara. Collector Quest 2000 Toy, Car & Action Figure Show. Marriott, Great America Pky. Exit 3 mi. N. of San Jose on the 101 Fwy. SH: 11am-4pm, T: 100, A: $5., $3. children, kids 5 & under free. PH: 831-454-1857.

Jan 22 2000 CA, San Mateo. Doll & Teddy Bear Show. Cty. Expo Ctr. SH: 10am-3:30pm. Lloyd Hogan, 5621 Glencrest Ln., Orangevale, CA 95662. PH: 916-989-9291.

Jan 23 2000 CA, Los Angeles. Comic Book & Science Fiction Convention. Shrine Auditorium Expo Ctr., 700 W. 32nd St. SH: 10am-5pm, A: $5. Bruce Schwartz, 2319-A W. Olive Ave., Burbank, CA 91506. PH: 818-954-8432.

Jan 23 2000 CA, Stanton-Orange County. NASCAR, NHRA, Hot Wheels & Toys Coll. Show. Rack & Cue Billiards, 7520 Katella Ave. SH: 9am-2:30pm, A: $2., under 12 free. Ron, PH: 909-902-0217.

Feb 5 2000 CA, Culver City. Forever Young Antique & Collectible Doll & Bear Show. Veterans Memorial Bldg., 4117 Overland Ave. SH: 10am-3pm, A: $4. Sandy Kline, PH: 818-368-4648.

Feb 6 2000 CA, Petaluma. Pollyanna Doll Show. Veterans Memorial Bldg., 1094 Petaluma Blvd. S. SH: 10am-4pm, A: $4., under 12 free. Paula Huber, PH: 707-763-5237.

Feb 12 2000 CA, Pleasanton. Doll Show & Teddy Bear Jamboree. Alameda Cty. Fairgrounds, Fwy. 680 S. off at Bernal. SH: 9am-4pm. Lloyd Hogan, 5621 Glencrest Ln., Orangevale, CA 95662. PH: 916-989-9291.

Feb 19 2000 CA, San Diego. Doll Show. Scottish Rite Ctr., 1895 Camino del Rio South, Exit I-8 at Mission Center Rd. SH: 10am-3pm, A: $5., children free. Christie Wright, PH: 619-560-5043 or Ruth Johnson, PH: 619-222-5335.

Feb 19-20 2000 CA, San Mateo. Toys, Antique & Collectors' Revival. Expo Center. SH: Sat. 9am-7pm, Sun. 10am-5pm. PH: 707-942-5079.

Mar 5 2000 CA, Sacramento. Antique Toy Show. Scottish Rite Temple, 6151 H St. SH: 10am-3pm. Wayne Gateley Productions, PO Box 221052, Sacramento, CA 95822. PH: 916-448-2655.

Mar 12 2000 CA, San Mateo. Barbie & Other Fashion Dolls Show. Cty. Expo Ctr., Fwy. 92 off at Delaware. SH: 10am-3:30pm. Lloyd Hogan, 5621 Glencrest Ln., Orangevale, CA 95662. PH: 916-989-9291.

Mar 25 2000 CA, Dixon. Doll & Bear Show. Mayfair Fairgrounds, Fwy. 80 to Hwy. 113 S. 2.5 mi. SH: 10am-3pm. Lloyd Hogan, 5621 Glencrest Ln., Orangevale, CA 95662. PH: 916-989-9291.

May 6 2000 CA, San Mateo. Doll & Teddy Bear Show. Cty. Expo Ctr. SH: 10am-3:30pm. Lloyd Hogan, 5621 Glencrest Ln., Orangevale, CA 95662. PH: 916-989-9291.

May 7 2000 CA, Hayward. Antique Toy Show. Centennial Hall, 22292 Foothill Blvd. SH: 10am-3pm. Wayne Gateley Productions, PO Box 221052, Sacramento, CA 95822. PH: 916-448-2655.

May 20 2000 CA, Pasadena. Forever Young Antique & Collectible Doll Show. Elks Lodge, 400 W. Colorado Blvd. SH: 10am-3pm, A: $4. Sandy Kline, PH: 818-368-4648.

Aug 12-13 2000 CA, San Diego. Teddy Bear, Doll & Antique Toy Show. Scottish Rite Ctr., 1895 Camino Del Rio S. SH: Sat. 10:30am-4pm, Sun. 10am-3pm, A: $5. Linda Mullins, PO Box 2327, Carlsbad, CA 92018. PH: 760-434-7444 or FAX: 760-434-0154.

Oct 14 2000 CA, Pasadena. Forever Young Antique & Collectible Doll Show. Elks Lodge, 400 W. Colorado Blvd. SH: 10am-3pm, A: $4. Sandy Kline, PH: 818-368-4648.

Nov 5 2000 CA, Hayward. Antique Toy Show. Centennial Hall, 22292 Foothill Blvd. SH: 10am-3pm. Wayne Gateley Productions, PO Box 221052, Sacramento, CA 95822. PH: 916-448-2655.

Nov 12 2000 CA, Sacramento. Antique Toy Show. Scottish Rite Temple, 6151 H St. SH: 10am-3pm. Wayne Gateley Productions, PO Box 221052, Sacramento, CA 95822. PH: 916-448-2655.

Nov 13 2000 CA, Sacramento. Pokemon Convention & Collectibles Show. Scottish Rite Temple, 6151 H St. SH: 10am-4pm, T: 110, A: $2. PH: 916-428-5600 or 707-422-3974.

CONNECTICUT

Jan 8 2000 CT, Meriden. Beanie Baby & Sports Card Show. Platt High School, 220 Coe Ave. SH: 9:30am-3pm, T: 60-6', A: $.99, under 12 free. Ernestin Schaper, PH: 203-634-0069.

Jan 9 2000 CT, Wallingford. Antique & Collectible Toy Show. Zandri's Stillwood Inn, Rt. 5, Exit 13, I-91. SH: 9am-2pm, A: $3. Little Rigger Toy Shows, PH: 860-582-2939.

Jan 16 2000 CT, Norwich. S.E. CT Toy & Collectible Show. Ramada Hotel, 395 to Exit 80. SH: 9am-3pm, T: 100, A: $4. Jim Arpin, 104 Kinsman Rd., Lisbon, CT 06351. PH: 860-822-8514.

Jan 16 2000 CT, Waterbury. Train Show. Four Points Hotel, 3580 E. Main St., Rt. 84 E. Exit 25A, Rt. 84 W. Exit 26. SH: 9am-3pm, A: $4., 12 & under free. Classic Shows, LLC, PO Box 2415, Shelton, CT 06484. PH: 203-926-1327.

Feb 4-6 2000 CT, Danbury. Triple Play Toy, Sports Card, Comic Book & Collectible Toy Show. Fair Mall, Rts. 84 & 7. SH: mall hrs., T: 75-8', A: free. F & B Sport Cards, Inc., Ferdinand Parascandolo, 482 Retford Ave., SI, NY 10306. PH: 718-667-9588 or 967-9172.

Feb 5 2000 CT, Meriden. Beanie Baby & Sports Card Show. Platt High School, 220 Coe Ave. SH: 9:30am-3pm, T: 60-6', A: $.99, under 12 free. Ernestin Schaper, PH: 203-634-0069.

Feb 13 2000 CT, Wallingford. Train Show. Zandri's Stillwood Inn, 1074 S. Colony Rd., US Rt. 5, Exit 13 on I-91. SH: 9am-2pm, A: $4., 12 & under free. Classic Shows, LLC, PO Box 2415, Shelton, CT 06484. PH: 203-926-1327.

Feb 20 2000 CT, Norwich. S.E. CT Toy & Collectible Show. Ramada Hotel, 395 to Exit 80. SH: 9am-3pm, T: 100, A: $4. Jim Arpin, 104 Kinsman Rd., Lisbon, CT 06351. PH: 860-822-8514.

Feb 27 2000 CT, Waterbury. A&M Collectible Toy Show. Sheraton, 3580 E. Main St., I-84W Exit 26, I 84E Exit 25A. SH: 9am-2pm, T: 100-8', A: $4., 8 & under free. Bernie, PH/FAX: 860-274-9592.

Mar 4 2000 CT, Meriden. Beanie Baby & Sports Card Show. Platt High School, 220 Coe Ave. SH: 9:30am-3pm, T: 60-6', A: $.99, under 12 free. Ernestin Schaper, PH: 203-634-0069.

Mar 12 2000 CT, Wallingford. Antique & Collectible Toy Show. Zandri's Stillwood Inn, Rt. 5, Exit 13, I-91. SH: 9am-2pm, A: $3. Little Rigger Toy Shows, PH: 860-582-2939.

Mar 12 2000 CT, Fairfield. Station Stop 2000 Housatonic Model Railroad. Rodger Ludlow Middle School, 785 Unquowa Rd. SH: 10am-4pm, T: 100. Jeff Dean, PH: 203-255-3795 Fri. 7pm-10pm.

Apr 1 2000 CT, Meriden. Beanie Baby & Sports Card Show. Platt High School, 220 Coe Ave. SH: 9:30am-3pm, T: 60-6', A: $.99, under 12 free. Ernestin Schaper, PH: 203-634-0069.

Apr 29 2000 CT, Kent. 27th Annual Doll Show. Community Ctr., Rt. 7. SH: 10am-3:30pm, A: $4. Carol Stanley, PH: 914-832-9626.

May 5-6 2000 CT, Stamford. Northeast PEZ Collectors Gathering. Sheraton, 2701 Summer St. SH: 10am-3pm, T: 100, A: $5. Richard Belyski, PO Box 124, Sea Cliff, NY 11579. PH: 516-676-1183.

May 13 2000 CT, Meriden. Beanie Baby & Sports Card Show. Platt High School, 220 Coe Ave. SH: 9:30am-3pm, T: 60-6', A: $.99, under 12 free. Ernestin Schaper, PH: 203-634-0069.

Jun 2-4 2000 CT, Danbury. Triple Play Toy, Sports Card, Comic Book & Collectible Toy Show. Fair Mall, Rts. 84 & 7. SH: mall hrs., T: 75-8', A: free. F & B Sport Cards, Inc., Ferdinand Parascandolo, 482 Retford Ave., SI, NY 10306. PH: 718-667-9588 or 967-9172.

Jun 3 2000 CT, Meriden. Beanie Baby & Sports Card Show. Platt High School, 220 Coe Ave. SH: 9:30am-3pm, T: 60-6', A: $.99, under 12 free. Ernestin Schaper, PH: 203-634-0069.

Sep 15-17 2000 CT, Danbury. Triple Play Toy,

Sports Card, Comic Book & Collectible Toy Show. Fair Mall, Rts. 84 & 7. SH: mall hrs., T: 75-8', A: free. F & B Sport Cards, Inc., Ferdinand Parascandolo, 482 Retford Ave., SI, NY 10306. PH: 718-667-9588 or 967-9172.

FLORIDA
Jan 8-9 2000 FL, Sarasota. Annual Salute to Racing. Fairgrounds. SH: 10am-6pm, A: $5., $3. ages 6-12, under 6 free. PH: 941-351-2411.

Jan 9 2000 FL, Ft. Lauderdale. Toy Show. Airport Hilton, 1870 Griffen Rd. SH: 10am-3pm, A: $5., $2. under 12. Marl, PH: 941-751-6275 or Joe, PH: 323-953-6490.

Jan 15-16 2000 FL, Orlando. 11th Annual Florida Extravaganza Collectible Toy Show FX 2000. Orange Cty. Convention Ctr., 9800 International Dr. T: 1,200. Marz Productions, PH: 941-343-0094.

Jan 15 2000 FL, Deland. Central FL Farm Toy Show. Fairgrounds, 3150 E. New York, Hwy. 44 Ave. SH: 9am-4pm, T: 100, A: $2., under 12 free. John Rammacher, 1610 Park Ave., Orange City, FL 32763. PH: 904-775-2891.

Jan 15-16 2000 FL, Jacksonville. Greenberg's Great Train & Collectible Toy Show. Fairgrounds, 510 Fairgrounds Place. SH: Sat. 11am-5pm, Sun. 11am-4pm, A: $6., $2. ages 6-12, under 6 free. Greenberg Shows, 7566 Main St., Sykesville, MD 21784. PH: 410-795-7447.

Jan 22 2000 FL, Ft. Lauderdale. South Florida Collectible Toy & Doll Super Show. Elks Exhibition Center, 700 NE 10th St., Pompano Beach. SH: 10am-5pm, T: 150-8'. Mark Leinberger, PH: 561-694-7982 or Jon Jacobus, PH: 954-772-1420.

Jan 22 2000 FL, Pompano Beach. 25th Annual Doll, Bear & Toy Show. Civic Ctr., 1801 NE 6th St. SH: 10am-4pm, A: $3., under 12 free. PH: 305-652-8237.

Jan 22-23 2000 FL, Tampa. Greenberg's Great Train & Collectible Toy Show. State Fairgrounds, 4800 US Hwy. 301 N. SH: Sat. 11am-5pm, Sun. 11am-4pm, A: $6., $2. ages 6-12, under 6 free. Greenberg Shows, 7566 Main St., Sykesville, MD 21784. PH: 410-795-7447.

Jan 28-29 2000 FL, Orlando. 3rd Annual FL Raggedy Ann, Doll & Teddy Bear Convention. Bahia Shrine Auditorium, 2300 Pembrook Dr. Larry Vaughan, 6337 Nightwind Cir., Orlando, FL 32818. PH: 407-884-5483.

Jan 29-30 2000 FL, Palmetto. Doll, Bear & Beanie Show. Manatee Civic Ctr., US Hwy. 41. SH: Sat. 9am-4pm, Sun. 11am-4pm, A: $3.50, $2. children. PH: 941-722-6675 or 727-796-9412.

Jan 29-30 2000 FL, Pompano Beach. Greenberg's Great Train & Collectible Toy Show. Omni-Broward Community College, 1000 Coconut Creek Blvd. SH: Sat. 11am-5pm, Sun. 11am-4pm, A: $6., $2. ages 6-12, under 6 free. Greenberg Shows, 7566 Main St., Sykesville, MD 21784. PH: 410-795-7447.

Feb 6 2000 FL, West Palm Beach. 6th Annual Toy Soldier & Action Figure Show. Airport Holiday Inn, 1301 Belvedere Rd. SH: 9am-3pm, T: 105, A: $5., $2. under 12. Frank Burns, 715 SW 15th St., Boynton Beach, FL 33426. PH: 561-732-7295.

Feb 6 2000 FL, Miami. Antique Toy, Doll & Collectibles Show. Airport Marriott Hotel, 1201 NW LeJeune Rd. SH: 10am-4pm, A: $5. PH: 305-446-4488 or 669-2550.

Feb 12-13 2000 FL, Lakeland. Central FL Toy & Collectible Expo. USA Speedway, Hwy. 33, Exit 20 off I-4. SP: 8am-4pm, T: 800, A: $3. Tom Conolly, 1056 Winifred Way, Lakeland, FL 33809. PH: 941-859-2180.

Feb 26 2000 FL, Boynton Beach. NASCAR, Hot Wheels & Collectibles Show. Holiday Inn Express, 480 Boynton Beach Blvd. SH: 10am-3pm, A: $2., under 12 free. Kevin Sansbury, 1127 Lake Geneva Dr., Lake Worth, FL 33461. PH: 561-547-0094.

Mar 4-5 2000 FL, Orlando. Collectible Toy & Doll Super Show. Bahia Shrine Auditorium, 2300 Pembrook Dr. SH: 10am-4pm, T: 200-8'. Mark Leinberger, PH: 561-694-7982 or Jon Jacobus, PH: 954-772-1420.

Mar 4 2000 FL, Jacksonville. River City Antique Doll, Bear & Collectible Show. Morocco Temple, St. Johns Bluff Rd. SH: 10am-4pm, A: $4., $1. under 10. M. Hill, 13030 Bent Pine Ct., E. Jacksonville, FL 32246. PH: 904-221-1235.

Mar 11-12 2000 FL, Ft. Lauderdale. Tate's Comic's Mondo Pop Collectible Show. War Memorial Auditorium, 800 NE 8th St. SH: 10am-5pm, A: $5. Tony or Tate, PH: 954-748-0181.

Mar 31-Apr 2 2000 FL, Orlando. Megacon 2000. Expo Ctr., 500 W. Livingston St. SH: Fri. 1pm-7pm, Sat. & Sun. 10am-6pm, 300 booths. Beth Widera, PH: 813-891-1702.

Oct 14-15 2000 FL, Deland. Tic Tac Toy Show. Volusia Cty. Fairgrounds, 3150 E. New York Ave. SH: Sat. 9am-5pm, Sun. 9am-4pm, T: 240. Allen Stone, 2088 Altoona Ln., Deltona, FL 32738. PH: 904-789-8464 or Bill Holcomb, PH: 407-668-9956.

GEORGIA
Jan 8-9 2000 GA, Norcross. Greenberg's Great Train & Collectible Toy Show. North Atlanta Trade Ctr., 1700 Jeurgens Ct. SH: Sat. 11am-5pm, Sun. 11am-4pm, A: $6., $2. ages 6-12, under 6 free. Greenberg Shows, 7566 Main St., Sykesville, MD 21784. PH: 410-795-7447.

Apr 9 2000 GA, Atlanta. Toy Show. Airport Marriott, 4700 Best Rd., College Park. SH: 10am-3pm, A: $5., $2. under 12. Marl, PH: 941-751-6275 or Joe, PH: 323-953-6490.

ILLINOIS
Jan 8 2000 IL, Orland Park. Toys, Diecast, Comic Books & Card Show. Civic Ctr., 1 blk. W. of LaGrange Rd. at 147th St. SH: 9am-3pm, T: 80. John Leary, 9522 W. Shore Dr., Oak Lawn, IL 60453. PH: 708-423-1758.

Jan 8 2000 IL, Schaumburg. G.I. Joe Collectors Club Chicago Area Division. Township District Library, 130 S. Roselle Rd. SH: 12noon-2:30pm, A: free. Kevin Bolger, 510 N. Prospect Manor Ave., Mt. Prospect, IL 60056. PH: 847-577-8437.

Jan 9 2000 IL, Bridgeview. If Its Got Wheels. John A Oremus Community Ctr., 7900 S. Oketo Ave. SH: 8am-2pm, A: $3., under 10 free. Jim LaCoco, 231 Englewood Ave., Bellwood, IL 60104. PH: 708-544-1975.

Jan 23 2000 IL, Rockford. Hot Wheels, NASCAR, Matchbox, Ertl & Diecast Show. Hoffman House at Holiday Inn, 7550 E. State St. (I-90, Exit Bus. 20). Russ Bambino, PH: 815-961-1223.

Jan 23 2000 IL, Orland Park.

Toys, Diecast, Comic Books & Card Show. Civic Ctr., 1 blk. W. of LaGrange Rd. at 147th St. SH: 9am-3pm, T: 80. John Leary, 9522 W. Shore Dr., Oak Lawn, IL 60453. PH: 708-423-1758.

Jan 29-30 2000 IL, Collinsville. Greenberg's Great Train & Collectible Toy Show. Gateway Center, 1 Gateway Dr. SH: Sat. 11am-5pm, Sun. 11am-4pm, A: $6., $2. ages 6-12, under 6 free. Greenberg Shows, 7566 Main St., Sykesville, MD 21784. PH: 410-795-7447.

Feb 6 2000 IL, Orland Park. Toys, Diecast, Comic Books & Card Show. Civic Ctr., 1 blk. W. of LaGrange Rd. at 147th St. SH: 9am-3pm, T: 80. John Leary, 9522 W. Shore Dr., Oak Lawn, IL 60453. PH: 708-423-1758.

Feb 12 2000 IL, Schaumburg. G.I. Joe Collectors Club Chicago Area Division. Township District Library, 130 S. Roselle Rd. SH: 12noon-2:30pm, A: free. Kevin Bolger, 510 N. Prospect Manor Ave., Mt. Prospect, IL 60056. PH: 847-577-8437.

Feb 20 2000 IL, Rockford. Hot Wheels, NASCAR, Matchbox, Ertl & Diecast Show. Hoffman House at Holiday Inn, 7550 E. State St. (I-90, Exit Bus. 20). Russ Bambino, PH: 815-961-1223.

Feb 20 2000 IL, Orland Park. Toys, Diecast, Comic Books & Card Show. Civic Ctr., 1 blk.

W. of LaGrange Rd. at 147th St. SH: 9am-3pm, T: 80. John Leary, 9522 W. Shore Dr., Oak Lawn, IL 60453. PH: 708-423-1758.

Feb 27 2000 IL, Wheaton. 35th Illinois Plastic Kit & Toy Show. Dupage Cty. Fairgrounds, Exhibition Ctr., 2015 W. Manchester Rd. SH: 9am-3pm, A: $4., $2. under 12. Past-Time Hobbies, Inc., PH: 630-969-1847.

Feb 27 2000 IL, Bridgeview. Toys, Die Cast, Comics, Beanies, Cards & More Show. Oremus Ctr., 2 blks. W. of Harlem Ave. at 79th St. SH: 9am-3pm, T: 65, A: $2.John Leary, 9522 W. Shore Dr., Oak Lawn, IL 60453. PH: 708-423-1758.

Mar 11 2000 IL, Schaumburg. G.I. Joe Collectors Club Chicago Area Division. Township District Library, 130 S. Roselle Rd. SH: 12noon-2:30pm, A: free. Kevin Bolger, 510 N. Prospect Manor Ave., Mt. Prospect, IL 60056. PH: 847-577-8437.

Mar 12 2000 IL, Rockford. Hot Wheels, NASCAR, Matchbox, Ertl & Diecast Show. Hoffman House at Holiday Inn, 7550 E. State St. (I-90, Exit Bus. 20). Russ Bambino, PH: 815-961-1223.

Mar 18 2000 IL, Schiller Park. 10th Annual Strictly 43rd Model Expo & Contest. Four Points Hotel by Sheraton-Chicago O'Hare, Mannheim & Irving Park Rds. SH: 8:30am-3pm, T: 75, A: $4. Don Anderson, PH: 630-964-6101.

Mar 19 2000 IL, Orland Park. Toys, Diecast, Comic Books & Card Show. Civic Ctr., 1 blk. W. of LaGrange Rd. at 147th St. SH: 9am-3pm, T: 80. John Leary, 9522 W. Shore Dr., Oak Lawn, IL 60453. PH: 708-423-1758.

Mar 26 2000 IL, Rosemont. Barbie Goes to... Chicago Show. Hotel Sofitel, 5550 N. River Rd. SH: 10am-4pm, A: $5., $2. under 12. Marl, PH: 941-751-6275 or Joe, PH: 213-953-6490.

Apr 2 2000 IL, Rockford. Hot Wheels, NASCAR, Matchbox, Ertl & Diecast Show. Hoffman House at Holiday Inn, 7550 E. State St. (I-90, Exit Bus. 20). Russ Bambino, PH: 815-961-1223.

Apr 2 2000 IL, Orland Park. Toys, Diecast, Comic Books & Card Show. Civic Ctr., 1 blk. W. of LaGrange Rd. at 147th St. SH: 9am-3pm, T: 80. John Leary, 9522 W. Shore Dr., Oak Lawn, IL 60453. PH: 708-423-1758.

Apr 8 2000 IL, Schaumburg. G.I. Joe Collectors Club Chicago Area Division. Township District Library, 130 S. Roselle Rd. SH: 12noon-2:30pm, A: free. Kevin Bolger, 510 N. Prospect Manor Ave., Mt. Prospect, IL 60056. PH: 847-577-8437.

Apr 15 2000 IL, Orland Park. Toys, Diecast, Comic Books & Card Show. Civic Ctr., 1 blk. W. of LaGrange Rd. at 147th St. SH: 9am-3pm, T: 80. John Leary, 9522 W. Shore Dr., Oak Lawn, IL 60453. PH: 708-423-1758.

Apr 30 2000 IL, Bridgeview. Toys, Die Cast, Comics, Beanies, Cards & More Show. Oremus Ctr., 2 blks. W. of Harlem Ave. at 79th St. SH: 9am-3pm, T: 65, A: $2.John Leary, 9522 W. Shore Dr., Oak Lawn, IL 60453. PH: 708-423-1758.

May 7 2000 IL, Rockford. Hot Wheels, NASCAR, Matchbox, Ertl & Diecast Show. Hoffman House at Holiday Inn, 7550 E. State St. (I-90, Exit Bus. 20). Russ Bambino, PH: 815-961-1223.

May 13 2000 IL, Orland Park. Toys, Diecast, Comic Books & Card Show. Civic Ctr., 1 blk. W. of LaGrange Rd. at 147th St. SH: 9am-3pm, T: 80. John Leary, 9522 W. Shore Dr., Oak Lawn, IL 60453. PH: 708-423-1758.

May 13 2000 IL, Schaumburg. G.I. Joe Collectors Club Chicago Area Division. Township District Library, 130 S. Roselle Rd. SH: 12noon-2:30pm, A: free. Kevin Bolger, 510 N. Prospect Manor Ave., Mt. Prospect, IL 60056. PH: 847-577-8437.

May 28 2000 IL, Orland Park. Toys, Diecast,

Comic Books & Card Show. Civic Ctr., 1 blk. W. of LaGrange Rd. at 147th St. SH: 9am-3pm, T: 80. John Leary, 9522 W. Shore Dr., Oak Lawn, IL 60453. PH: 708-423-1758.

Jun 4 2000 IL, Rockford. Hot Wheels, NASCAR, Matchbox, Ertl & Diecast Show. Hoffman House at Holiday Inn, 7550 E. State St. (I-90, Exit Bus. 20). Russ Bambino, PH: 815-961-1223.

Jun 10 2000 IL, Schaumburg. G.I. Joe Collectors Club Chicago Area Division. Township District Library, 130 S. Roselle Rd. SH: 12noon-2:30pm, A: free. Kevin Bolger, 510 N. Prospect Manor Ave., Mt. Prospect, IL 60056. PH: 847-577-8437.

Jun 25 2000 IL, Orland Park. Toys, Diecast, Comic Books & Card Show. Civic Ctr., 1 blk. W. of LaGrange Rd. at 147th St. SH: 9am-3pm, T: 80. John Leary, 9522 W. Shore Dr., Oak Lawn, IL 60453. PH: 708-423-1758.

Jul 2 2000 IL, Rockford. Hot Wheels, NASCAR, Matchbox, Ertl & Diecast Show. Hoffman House at Holiday Inn, 7550 E. State St. (I-90, Exit Bus. 20). Russ Bambino, PH: 815-961-1223.

Jul 2 2000 IL, Chicago. McDonald's Collectors Club Show. Wyndham Northwest, 400 Park Blvd., Itasca. SH: 9am-3pm, T: 175, A: $3. Lee Lasseigne, PO Box 1212, Bolingbrook, IL 60440. PH: 630-739-5305.

Aug 6 2000 IL, Rockford. Hot Wheels, NASCAR, Matchbox, Ertl & Diecast Show. Hoffman House at Holiday Inn, 7550 E. State St. (I-90, Exit Bus. 20). Russ Bambino, PH: 815-961-1223.

Sep 10 2000 IL, Rockford. Hot Wheels, NASCAR, Matchbox, Ertl & Diecast Show. Hoffman House at Holiday Inn, 7550 E. State St. (I-90, Exit Bus. 20). Russ Bambino, PH: 815-961-1223.

Sep 30 2000 IL, Bridgeview. Toys, Die Cast, Comics, Beanies, Cards & More Show. Oremus Ctr., 2 blks. W. of Harlem Ave. at 79th St. SH: 9am-3pm, T: 65, A: $2.John Leary, 9522 W. Shore Dr., Oak Lawn, IL 60453. PH: 708-423-1758.

Oct 8 2000 IL, Rockford. Hot Wheels, NASCAR, Matchbox, Ertl & Diecast Show. Hoffman House at Holiday Inn, 7550 E. State St. (I-90, Exit Bus. 20). Russ Bambino, PH: 815-961-1223.

Nov 5 2000 IL, Rockford. Hot Wheels, NASCAR, Matchbox, Ertl & Diecast Show. Hoffman House at Holiday Inn, 7550 E. State St. (I-90, Exit Bus. 20). Russ Bambino, PH: 815-961-1223.

Dec 3 2000 IL, Rockford. Hot Wheels, NASCAR, Matchbox, Ertl & Diecast Show. Hoffman House at Holiday Inn, 7550 E. State St. (I-90, Exit Bus. 20). Russ Bambino, PH: 815-961-1223.

INDIANA

Jan 9 2000 IN, Indianapolis. Super Sunday Indy Automotive Swap Meet & Car Show. Indiana State Fairgrounds, West Pavilion. Mid America Promotions, 7322 S. Archer Rd., Justice, IL 60458. PH: 708-563-4300 9am-5pm.

IOWA

Mar 12 2000 IA, Maquoketa. 18th Annual Doll, Toy & Bear Show. Jackson Cty. Fairgrounds, Jct. Hwys. 62 & 64. SH: 9am-4pm, A: $2.50, under 10 free. Dora Pitts, 4697 155th St., Clinton, IA 52732. PH: 319-242-0139.

Apr 15 2000 IA, Des Moines. 12th Annual Doll, Toy & Bear Show. Soccer & Sports Ctr., 5406 Merle Hay Rd., I-80, Exit 131 N. on Merle Hay Rd. SH: 9am-4pm, A: $3., under 10 free. Dora Pitts, 4697 155th St., Clinton, IA 52732. PH: 319-242-0139.

Nov 3-5 2000 IA, Dyersville. 23rd Annual National Farm Toy Show. PH: 800-533-8293.

KANSAS

Feb 27 2000 KS, Kansas City. Heartland Toy & Automobilia Show. Eisenhower Community Ctr., 2901 N. 72nd St. SH: 9am-3pm, T: 200, A: $2. Don Kimrey, 9700 E. 84th St., Raytown, MO 64138. PH: 816-353-6151.

Mar 12 2000 KS, Kansas City. 8th Annual Spring Toy Show. Jack Reardon Civic Ctr., 5th & Minnesota. SH: 10am-4pm, A: $3. Judy Condray, 1005 W. 11th, Concordia, KS 66901. PH: 785-243-3774.

May 6-7 2000 KS, White Cloud. Toys, Beanie Babies & Flea Market. Main St. SH: daylight to dark, A: free. Judy Woodruff, PO Box 84, White Cloud, KS 66094. PH: 785-595-3320.

MARYLAND

Jan 29 2000 MD, Baltimore. Greater Baltimore Antique & Collectible Toy Show. Tall Cedars Hall, 2501 Putty Hill Ave. SH: 9am-2pm, T: 200, A: $3. Raymond Bosley & David Hart, 3010 Merrymans Mill Rd., Phoenix, MD 21131. PH: 410-628-7972 or 433-4278.

Feb 12-13 2000 MD, Upper Marlboro. Greenberg's Great Train & Collectible Toy Show. The Show Place Arena, 14900 Pennsylvania Ave. SH: Sat. 11am-5pm, Sun. 11am-4pm, A: $6., $2. ages 6-12, under 6 free. Greenberg Shows, 7566 Main St., Sykesville, MD 21784. PH: 410-795-7447.

Mar 18-19 2000 MD, Timonium. Greenberg's Great Train & Collectible Toy Show. State Fairgrounds-Exhibition Hall, 2200 York Rd. SH: Sat. 11am-5pm, Sun. 11am-4pm, A: $6., $2. ages 6-12, under 6 free. Greenberg Shows, 7566 Main St., Sykesville, MD 21784. PH: 410-795-7447.

Mar 26 2000 MD, Chevy Chase. Toys & Collectibles Show. Leland Community Ctr., 4301 Willow Ln. SH: 10am-3pm, T: 25-6', A: free. Claron McDaniel, 4301 Willow Ln., Chevy Chase, MD 20815. PH: 301-652-2249.

Apr 8 2000 MD, Baltimore. Greater Baltimore Antique & Collectible Toy Show. Tall Cedars Hall, 2501 Putty Hill Ave. SH: 9am-2pm, T: 200, A: $3. Raymond Bosley & David Hart, 3010 Merrymans Mill Rd., Phoenix, MD 21131. PH: 410-628-7972 or 433-4278.

MASSACHUSETTS

Feb 13 2000 MA, Dedham. Annual Cabin Fever Show. Holiday Inn, Rt. 1, Exit 15A. SH: 9:30am-3pm, A: $4.50. Mrs. Devlin, PH: 508-379-9733.

Feb 13 2000 MA, South Attleboro. Toys, Comic Book, Non-Sport Cards & Coll. Show. K of C, 304 Highland Ave. SH: 10am-3pm. Harry Martin, 936 South St., Wrentham, MA 02093. PH: 508-384-8491.

Mar 19 2000 MA, Dedham. Annual Spring Show. Holiday Inn, Rt. 1, Exit 15A. SH: 9:30am-3pm, A: $4.50. Mrs. Devlin, PH: 508-379-9733.

Mar 26 2000 MA, South Attleboro. Toys, Comic Book, Non-Sport Cards & Coll. Show. K of C, 304 Highland Ave. SH: 10am-3pm. Harry Martin, 936 South St., Wrentham, MA 02093. PH: 508-384-8491.

May 7 2000 MA, South Attleboro. Toys, Comic Book, Non-Sport Cards & Coll. Show. K of C, 304 Highland Ave. SH: 10am-3pm. Harry Martin, 936 South St., Wrentham, MA 02093. PH: 508-384-8491.

Jun 25 2000 MA, South Attleboro. Toys, Comic Book, Non-Sport Cards & Coll. Show. K of C, 304 Highland Ave. SH: 10am-3pm. Harry Martin, 936 South St., Wrentham, MA 02093. PH: 508-384-8491.

Aug 13 2000 MA, South Attleboro. Toys, Comic Book, Non-Sport Cards & Coll. Show. K of C, 304 Highland Ave. SH: 10am-3pm. Harry Martin, 936 South St., Wrentham, MA 02093. PH: 508-384-8491.

Sep 24 2000 MA, South Attleboro. Toys, Comic Book, Non-Sport Cards & Coll. Show. K of C, 304 Highland Ave. SH: 10am-3pm. Harry Martin, 936 South St., Wrentham, MA 02093. PH: 508-384-8491.

Oct 15 2000 MA, South Attleboro. Toys, Comic Book, Non-Sport Cards & Coll. Show. K of C, 304 Highland Ave. SH: 10am-3pm. Harry Martin, 936 South St., Wrentham, MA 02093. PH: 508-384-8491.

Nov 12 2000 MA, South Attleboro. Toys, Comic Book, Non-Sport Cards & Coll. Show. K of C, 304 Highland Ave. SH: 10am-3pm. Harry Martin, 936 South St., Wrentham, MA 02093. PH: 508-384-8491.

Dec 17 2000 MA, South Attleboro. Toys, Comic Book, Non-Sport Cards & Coll. Show. K of C, 304 Highland Ave. SH: 10am-3pm. Harry Martin, 936 South St., Wrentham, MA 02093. PH: 508-384-8491.

MICHIGAN

Jan 9 2000 MI, Troy. Antique Toy Show. A.P.C.C. Hall, 15 Mile & Dequindre Rd., 2975 E. Maple Rd. SH: 10am-3pm, T: 135, A: $4., under 12 free. Kevin Hauser, 248 S. Adams, Birmingham, MI 48009. PH: 248-642-1043.

Jan 9 2000 MI, Saginaw. Toy, Beanie Baby, Sports Card, Memorabilia & Comic Book Show. St. Vincent Home, 925 N. River Rd., btw. State Street & Gratiot Rd. SH: 9:30am-4pm. Rick Doud, PH: 517-754-0249.

Jan 15-16 2000 MI, Plymouth. Train & Toy Show. Cultural Center, 525 Farmer St. SH: Sat. 11am-5pm, Sun. 10am-4pm, A: $5., $2. ages 4-12. R.R. Promotions, Inc., PO Box 6094, Plymouth, MI 48170. PH/FAX: 734-455-2110.

Jan 30 2000 MI, Madison Hgts. 43rd Detroit Toy Collectors Exposition. United Food & Comm. Workers Union Bldg., 876 Horace Brown Dr. (I-75 & 13 Mile). SH: 10am-2pm. Old Toyland Shows, John Carlisle, PO Box 1007, Lockport, NY 14095.

Feb 6 2000 MI, Saginaw. Toy, Beanie Baby, Sports Card, Memorabilia & Comic Book Show. St. Vincent Home, 925 N. River Rd., btw. State Street & Gratiot Rd. SH: 9:30am-4pm. Rick Doud, PH: 517-754-0249.

Feb 13 2000 MI, Plymouth. We Love Barbie Fashion Doll Show. Cultural Center, 525 Farmer St. SH: 11am-4pm, A: $5., $2. ages 4-12. R.R. Promotions, Inc., PO Box 6094, Plymouth, MI 48170. PH/FAX: 734-455-2110.

Mar 5 2000 MI, Saginaw. Toy, Beanie Baby, Sports Card, Memorabilia & Comic Book Show. St. Vincent Home, 925 N. River Rd., btw. State Street & Gratiot Rd. SH: 9:30am-4pm. Rick Doud, PH: 517-754-0249.

Apr 2 2000 MI, Madison Hgts. 44th Detroit Toy Collectors Exposition. United Food & Comm. Workers Union Bldg., 876 Horace Brown Dr. (I-75 & 13 Mile). SH: 10am-2pm. Old Toyland Shows, John Carlisle, PO Box 1007, Lockport, NY 14095.

Apr 9 2000 MI, Saginaw. Toy, Beanie Baby, Sports Card, Memorabilia & Comic Book Show. St. Vincent Home, 925 N. River Rd., btw. State Street & Gratiot Rd. SH: 9:30am-4pm. Rick Doud, PH: 517-754-0249.

Aug 6 2000 MI, Madison Hgts. 45th Detroit Toy Collectors Exposition. United Food & Comm. Workers Union Bldg., 876 Horace Brown Dr. (I-75 & 13 Mile). SH: 10am-2pm. Old Toyland Shows, John Carlisle, PO Box 1007, Lockport, NY 14095.

Nov 5 2000 MI, Madison Hgts. 46th Detroit Toy Collectors Exposition. United Food & Comm. Workers Union Bldg., 876 Horace Brown Dr. (I-75 & 13 Mile). SH: 10am-2pm. Old Toyland Shows, John Carlisle, PO Box 1007, Lockport, NY 14095.

MINNESOTA

Jan 16 2000 MN, Brooklyn Center. 19th Annual Winter Doll, Bear & Miniature Show. Earle Brown Heritage Ctr., 6155 Earle Brown Dr. (I-694 & Hwy. 100). SH: 10am-4pm, A: $3.50, $1. under 12. Carol's Doll House, 10761 University Ave. NE, Blaine, MN 55434.

PH: 612-755-7475.

Mar 12 2000 MN, Minneapolis. Antique, Modern & Collectible Toys, Dolls & Bears Show. Medina Ballroom, 500 Hwy. 55 (4 mi. W. of 494 on Hwy. 55). SH: 9:30am-2:30pm, A: $3., under 12 free with adult. Vicki Johanneck, 1727 Pulaski Rd., Buffalo, MN 55313. PH: 612-682-0168 or FAX: 612-682-3168.

Nov 12 2000 MN, Minneapolis. Antique, Modern & Collectible Toys, Dolls & Bears Show. Medina Ballroom, 500 Hwy. 55 (4 mi. W. of 494 on Hwy. 55). SH: 9:30am-2:30pm, A: $3., under 12 free with adult. Vicki Johanneck, 1727 Pulaski Rd., Buffalo, MN 55313. PH: 612-682-0168 or FAX: 612-682-3168.

MISSOURI

Feb 4-6 2000 MO, St. Louis. Gateway Mid-America Toy Show. Airport Holiday Inn, I-70 & Lindbergh. SH: Fri. 12noon-9pm, Sat. 9am-9pm, Sun. 9am-3pm, T: 300. Roy Lee Baker, RR 1, Box 88, Shipman, IL 62685. PH: 618-836-7787.

NEBRASKA

Jan 16 2000 NE, Omaha. Toy, Coin & BB Card Show. Holiday Inn, I-80 72nd St. SH: 10am-4pm, T: 100-6', A: free. Dave Fogleman, PO Box 241668, Omaha, NE 68124. PH: 402-297-7857.

Feb 20 2000 NE, Omaha. Toy, Coin & BB Card Show. Holiday Inn, I-80 72nd St. SH: 10am-4pm, T: 100-6', A: free. Dave Fogleman, PO Box 241668, Omaha, NE 68124. PH: 402-297-7857.

Mar 19 2000 NE, Omaha. Toy, Coin & BB Card Show. Holiday Inn, I-80 72nd St. SH: 10am-4pm, T: 100-6', A: free. Dave Fogleman, PO Box 241668, Omaha, NE 68124. PH: 402-297-7857.

Apr 16 2000 NE, Omaha. Toy, Coin & BB Card Show. Holiday Inn, I-80 72nd St. SH: 10am-4pm, T: 100-6', A: free. Dave Fogleman, PO Box 241668, Omaha, NE 68124. PH: 402-297-7857.

May 14 2000 NE, Omaha. Toy, Coin & BB Card Show. Holiday Inn, I-80 72nd St. SH: 10am-4pm, T: 100-6', A: free. Dave Fogleman, PO Box 241668, Omaha, NE 68124. PH: 402-297-7857.

Jun 18 2000 NE, Omaha. Toy, Coin & BB Card Show. Holiday Inn, I-80 72nd St. SH: 10am-4pm, T: 100-6', A: free. Dave Fogleman, PO Box 241668, Omaha, NE 68124. PH: 402-297-7857.

Jul 9 2000 NE, Omaha. Toy, Coin & BB Card Show. Holiday Inn, I-80 72nd St. SH: 10am-4pm, T: 100-6', A: free. Dave Fogleman, PO Box 241668, Omaha, NE 68124. PH: 402-297-7857.

Aug 27 2000 NE, Omaha. Toy, Coin & BB Card Show. Holiday Inn, I-80 72nd St. SH: 10am-4pm, T: 100-6', A: free. Dave Fogleman, PO Box 241668, Omaha, NE 68124. PH: 402-297-7857.

Sep 10 2000 NE, Omaha. Toy, Coin & BB Card Show. Holiday Inn, I-80 72nd St. SH: 10am-4pm, T: 100-6', A: free. Dave Fogleman, PO Box 241668, Omaha, NE 68124. PH: 402-297-7857.

Oct 29 2000 NE, Omaha. Toy, Coin & BB Card Show. Holiday Inn, I-80 72nd St. SH: 10am-4pm, T: 100-6', A: free. Dave Fogleman, PO Box 241668, Omaha, NE 68124. PH: 402-297-7857.

Nov 19 2000 NE, Omaha. Toy, Coin & BB Card Show. Holiday Inn, I-80 72nd St. SH: 10am-4pm, T: 100-6', A: free. Dave Fogleman, PO Box 241668, Omaha, NE 68124. PH: 402-297-7857.

Dec 17 2000 NE, Omaha. Toy, Coin & BB Card Show. Holiday Inn, I-80 72nd St. SH: 10am-4pm, T: 100-6', A: free. Dave Fogleman, PO Box 241668, Omaha, NE 68124. PH: 402-297-7857.

NEVADA

Feb 27 2000 NV, Las Vegas. Toy Show. Gold Coast, 4000 W. Flamingo Rd. SH: 10am-3pm, A: $5., $2. under 12. Marl, PH: 941-751-6275 or Joe, PH: 323-953-6490.

NEW HAMPSHIRE

Jan 9 2000 NH, Salem. Beanie Baby, Sports Card & Pokemon Show. Elks Hall, Rt. 111. SH: 9am-2pm, T: 40, A: $1., under 9 free. Bob Larocque, PH: 603-880-7528.

Jan 23 2000 NH, Salem. Beanie Baby, Sports Card & Pokemon Show. Elks Hall, Rt. 111. SH: 9am-2pm, T: 40, A: $1., under 9 free. Bob Larocque, PH: 603-880-7528.

Feb 6 2000 NH, Salem. Beanie Baby, Sports Card & Pokemon Show. Elks Hall, Rt. 111. SH: 9am-2pm, T: 40, A: $1., under 9 free. Bob Larocque, PH: 603-880-7528.

Feb 20 2000 NH, Salem. Beanie Baby, Sports Card & Pokemon Show. Elks Hall, Rt. 111. SH: 9am-2pm, T: 40, A: $1., under 9 free. Bob Larocque, PH: 603-880-7528.

Mar 5 2000 NH, Salem. Beanie Baby, Sports Card & Pokemon Show. Elks Hall, Rt. 111. SH: 9am-2pm, T: 40, A: $1., under 9 free. Bob Larocque, PH: 603-880-7528.

Mar 19 2000 NH, Salem. Beanie Baby, Sports Card & Pokemon Show. Elks Hall, Rt. 111. SH: 9am-2pm, T: 40, A: $1., under 9 free. Bob Larocque, PH: 603-880-7528.

Apr 2 2000 NH, Salem. Beanie Baby, Sports Card & Pokemon Show. Elks Hall, Rt. 111. SH: 9am-2pm, T: 40, A: $1., under 9 free. Bob Larocque, PH: 603-880-7528.

Apr 16 2000 NH, Salem. Beanie Baby, Sports Card & Pokemon Show. Elks Hall, Rt. 111. SH: 9am-2pm, T: 40, A: $1., under 9 free. Bob Larocque, PH: 603-880-7528.

May 21 2000 NH, Salem. Beanie Baby, Sports Card & Pokemon Show. Elks Hall, Rt. 111. SH: 9am-2pm, T: 40, A: $1., under 9 free. Bob Larocque, PH: 603-880-7528.

Jun 4 2000 NH, Salem. Beanie Baby, Sports Card & Pokemon Show. Elks Hall, Rt. 111. SH: 9am-2pm, T: 40, A: $1., under 9 free. Bob Larocque, PH: 603-880-7528.

Aug 13 2000 NH, Salem. Beanie Baby, Sports Card & Pokemon Show. Elks Hall, Rt. 111. SH: 9am-2pm, T: 40, A: $1., under 9 free. Bob Larocque, PH: 603-880-7528.

Sep 10 2000 NH, Salem. Beanie Baby, Sports Card & Pokemon Show. Elks Hall, Rt. 111. SH: 9am-2pm, T: 40, A: $1., under 9 free. Bob Larocque, PH: 603-880-7528.

Oct 8 2000 NH, Salem. Beanie Baby, Sports Card & Pokemon Show. Elks Hall, Rt. 111. SH: 9am-2pm, T: 40, A: $1., under 9 free. Bob Larocque, PH: 603-880-7528.

Oct 22 2000 NH, Salem. Beanie Baby, Sports Card & Pokemon Show. Elks Hall, Rt. 111. SH: 9am-2pm, T: 40, A: $1., under 9 free. Bob Larocque, PH: 603-880-7528.

Nov 5 2000 NH, Salem. Beanie Baby, Sports Card & Pokemon Show. Elks Hall, Rt. 111. SH: 9am-2pm, T: 40, A: $1., under 9 free. Bob Larocque, PH: 603-880-7528.

Nov 19 2000 NH, Salem. Beanie Baby, Sports Card & Pokemon Show. Elks Hall, Rt. 111. SH: 9am-2pm, T: 40, A: $1., under 9 free. Bob Larocque, PH: 603-880-7528.

Dec 3 2000 NH, Salem. Beanie Baby, Sports Card & Pokemon Show. Elks Hall, Rt. 111. SH: 9am-2pm, T: 40, A: $1., under 9 free. Bob Larocque, PH: 603-880-7528.

NEW JERSEY

Jan 1-2 2000 NJ, East Brunswick. Toys, Sports Cards & Collectibles Week-End. Ramada Inn, Rt. 18 S. at NJ Tpke. Exit 9. SH: Sat. 11am-5pm, Sun. 10am-4pm, T: 50, A: $2., under 6 free. Sallie Natowitz, PO Box 796, Matawan, NJ 07747. PH: 732-583-7915.

Jan 2 2000 NJ, East Hanover. The Big Toy Event. Ramada Hotel, 130 Rt. 10 W. SH: 10am-4pm, T: 125, A: $4., $1.50 children. PH: 570-620-2422.

Jan 8 2000 NJ, Colts Neck. Doll & Bear Show. Firehouse #2, Conover Rd., just off Rt. 34. SH: 10am-4pm, T: 8', A: $1.50, under 6 free. Sallie Natowitz, PO Box 796, Matawan, NJ 07747. PH/FAX: 732-583-7915.

Jan 16 2000 NJ, Wayne. Toy & Collectibles Show. Wayne Manor, 1515 State Route 23. SH: 9am-3pm, T: 80, A: $4., under 12 free. Phil De Mario, PO Box 4094, Wayne, NJ 07474. PH: 973-667-2112.

Jan 16 2000 NJ, East Hanover. Greater Northeast Doll & Teddy Bear Winter Expo Show. Ramada Hotel, 130 Rt. 10 W. SH: 10am-4pm, T: 150, A: $4., $1.50 children ages 6 & older. Heritage Promos., Yolanda Stanczyk, PO Box 368, Tannersville, PA 18372. PH: 570-620-2422.

Jan 16 2000 NJ, Somerset. Doll & Bear Show. Holiday Inn, 195 Davidson Ave. at I-287, Exit 10. SH: 10am-4pm, T: 6' & 8', A: $2.50, under 6 free. Sallie Natowitz, PO Box 796, Matawan, NJ 07747. PH/FAX: 732-583-7915.

Jan 21-23 2000 NJ, Freehold. Triple Play Toy, Comic Book, Sports Card, Memorabilia & Collectible Show. Raceway Mall, 3710 Route 9 (across from Freehold Race-track). SH: mall hrs., T: 100-8', A: free. F & B Sport Cards, Inc., Ferdinand Parascandolo, 482 Retford Ave., SI, NY 10306. PH: 718-667-9588 or 967-9172.

Feb 6 2000 NJ, Wayne. Toy & Collectibles Show. Co. #1 Firemen's Convention Ctr., 1 Parish Dr. off Rt. 23 North at Lincoln Park Exit. SH: 9am-3pm, T: 100-6', A: free. Phil De Mario, PO Box 4094, Wayne, NJ 07474. PH: 973-667-2112.

Feb 18-20 2000 NJ, East Brunswick. Triple Play Sports Card, Memorabilia, Beanie Baby, Comic Book & Collectible Toy Show. Brunswick Square Mall, 755 Rt. 18. SH: mall hrs., T: 65-8', A: free. F & B Promos., Ferdinand Parascandolo, 482 Retford Ave., SI, NY 10306. PH: 718-667-9588 or 967-9172.

Feb 20 2000 NJ, Princeton. Doll & Bear Show. Holiday Inn, 4355 Rt. 1 S. at Ridge Rd. SH: 10am-4pm, T: 6', A: $2., under 6 free. Sallie Natowitz, PO Box 796, Matawan, NJ 07747. PH/FAX: 732-583-7915.

Feb 27 2000 NJ, Mount Laurel. Doll & Bear Show. Radisson Hotel, 915 Rt. 73 at NJ Tpke., Exit 4. SH: 10am-4pm, T: 6', A: $2.50, under 6 free. Sallie Natowitz, PO Box 796, Matawan, NJ 07747. PH/FAX: 732-583-7915.

Mar 4-5 2000 NJ, Pennsauken. Greenberg's Great Train & Collectible Toy Show. South Jersey Expo Ctr., 2323 Rt. 73. SH: Sat. 11am-5pm, Sun. 11am-4pm, A: $6., $2. ages 6-12, under 6 free. Greenberg Shows, 7566 Main St., Sykesville, MD 21784. PH: 410-795-7447.

Mar 5 2000 NJ, Wayne. Toy & Collectibles Show. Co. #1 Firemen's Convention Ctr., 1 Parish Dr. off Rt. 23 North at Lincoln Park Exit. SH: 9am-3pm, T: 100-6', A: free. Phil De Mario, PO Box 4094, Wayne, NJ 07474. PH: 973-667-2112.

Mar 11-12 2000 NJ, Edison. Greenberg's Great Train & Collectible Toy Show. Convention Ctr.-Raritan Ctr., 97 Sunfield Ave. SH: Sat. 11am-5pm, Sun. 11am-4pm, A: $6., $2. ages 6-12, under 6 free. Greenberg Shows, 7566 Main St., Sykesville, MD 21784. PH: 410-795-7447.

Mar 12 2000 NJ, North Bergen. Toys, Collectibles & Memorabilia Show. Schuetzen Park Casino, 32nd St. & Kennedy Blvd. SH: 9am-3pm, T: 50, A: $5. Ed Gries, PO Box 572, Hackensack, NJ 07602. PH: 201-342-6475.

Mar 18 2000 NJ, Newark. International Mega Collectibles Show. Airport Sheraton Hotel, 128 Frontage Rd. SH: 9:30am-5pm, T: 300. K & S Promotions, 1020 Arlington Rd., New Milford, NJ 07646. PH: 201-261-4982, 261-8803 or FAX: 201-385-9291.

Mar 25-26 2000 NJ, Atlantic City. Spring Festival. Convention Center, One Ocean Way. SH: Sat. 10am-8pm, Sun. 10am-5pm. Brimfield Assoc., Inc., PO Box 1800, Ocean City, NJ 08226. PH: 609-926-1800.

Mar 25-26 2000 NJ, Hackensack. Greenberg's Great Train & Collectible Toy Show. Fairleigh-Dickenson Univ.-Rothman Athletic Ctr. SH: Sat. 11am-5pm, Sun. 11am-4pm, A: $6., $2. ages 6-12, under 6 free. Greenberg Shows, 7566 Main St., Sykesville, MD 21784. PH: 410-795-7447.

Mar 31-Apr 2 2000 NJ, Freehold. Triple Play Toy, Comic Book, Sports Card, Memorabilia & Collectible Show. Raceway Mall, 3710 Route 9 (across from Freehold Racetrack). SH: mall hrs., T: 100-8', A: free. F & B Sport Cards, Inc., Ferdinand Parascandolo, 482 Retford Ave., SI, NY 10306. PH: 718-667-9588 or 967-9172.

Apr 2 2000 NJ, Wayne. Toy & Collectibles Show. Co. #1 Firemen's Convention Ctr., 1 Parish Dr. off Rt. 23 North at Lincoln Park Exit. SH: 9am-3pm, T: 100-6', A: free. Phil De Mario, PO Box 4094, Wayne, NJ 07474. PH: 973-667-2112.

Apr 8 2000 NJ, Colts Neck. Doll & Bear Show. Firehouse #2, Conover Rd., just off Rt. 34. SH: 10am-4pm, T: 8', A: $1.50, under 6 free. Sallie Natowitz, PO Box 796, Matawan, NJ 07747. PH/FAX: 732-583-7915.

Apr 28-30 2000 NJ, East Brunswick. Triple Play Sports Card, Memorabilia, Beanie Baby, Comic Book & Collectible Toy Show. Brunswick Square Mall, 755 Rt. 18. SH: mall hrs., T: 65-8', A: free. F & B Promos., Ferdinand Parascandolo, 482 Retford Ave., SI, NY 10306. PH: 718-667-9588 or 967-9172.

May 7 2000 NJ, Wayne. Toy & Collectibles Show. Co. #1 Firemen's Convention Ctr., 1 Parish Dr. off Rt. 23 North at Lincoln Park Exit. SH: 9am-3pm, T: 100-6', A: free. Phil De Mario, PO Box 4094, Wayne, NJ 07474. PH: 973-667-2112.

Jun 4 2000 NJ, Wayne. Toy & Collectibles Show. Co. #1 Firemen's Convention Ctr., 1 Parish Dr. off Rt. 23 North at Lincoln Park Exit. SH: 9am-3pm, T: 100-6', A: free. Phil De Mario, PO Box 4094, Wayne, NJ 07474. PH: 973-667-2112.

Jun 4 2000 NJ, East Hanover. Greater Northeast Doll & Teddy Bear Summer Expo Show. Ramada Hotel, 130 Rt. 10 W. SH: 10am-4pm, T: 150, A: $4., $1.50 children ages 6 & older. Heritage Promotions, PO Box 368, Tannersville, PA 18372. PH: 570-620-2422.

Jul 2 2000 NJ, Wayne. Toy & Collectibles Show. Co. #1 Firemen's Convention Ctr., 1 Parish Dr. off Rt. 23 North at Lincoln Park Exit. SH: 9am-3pm, T: 100-6', A: free. Phil De Mario, PO Box 4094, Wayne, NJ 07474. PH: 973-667-2112.

Jul 22 2000 NJ, Newark. Barbie Doll & Fashion Doll Show. Holiday Inn North, 160 Frontage Rd. SH: 10am-3pm, A: $5., $2. under 12. Marl, PH: 941-751-6275 or Joe, PH: 323-953-6490.

Jul 28-30 2000 NJ, Freehold. Triple Play Toy, Comic Book, Sports Card, Memorabilia & Collectible Show. Raceway Mall, 3710 Route 9 (across from Freehold Racetrack). SH: mall hrs., T: 100-8', A: free. F & B Sport Cards, Inc., Ferdinand Parascandolo, 482 Retford Ave., SI, NY 10306. PH: 718-667-9588 or 967-9172.

Aug 6 2000 NJ, Wayne. Toy & Collectibles Show. Co. #1 Firemen's Convention Ctr., 1 Parish Dr. off Rt. 23 North at Lincoln Park Exit. SH: 9am-3pm, T: 100-6', A: free. Phil De Mario, PO Box 4094, Wayne, NJ 07474. PH: 973-667-2112.

Aug 25-27 2000 NJ, East Brunswick. Triple Play Sports Card, Memorabilia, Beanie Baby, Comic Book & Collectible Toy Show. Brunswick Square Mall, 755 Rt. 18. SH: mall hrs., T: 65-8', A: free. F & B Promos., Ferdinand Parascandolo, 482 Retford

Ave., SI, NY 10306. PH: 718-667-9588 or 967-9172.

Sep 3 2000 NJ, Wayne. Toy & Collectibles Show. Co. #1 Firemen's Convention Ctr., 1 Parish Dr. off Rt. 23 North at Lincoln Park Exit. SH: 9am-3pm, T: 100-6', A: free. Phil De Mario, PO Box 4094, Wayne, NJ 07474. PH: 973-667-2112.

Oct 1 2000 NJ, Wayne. Toy & Collectibles Show. Co. #1 Firemen's Convention Ctr., 1 Parish Dr. off Rt. 23 North at Lincoln Park Exit. SH: 9am-3pm, T: 100-6', A: free. Phil De Mario, PO Box 4094, Wayne, NJ 07474. PH: 973-667-2112.

Oct 20-22 2000 NJ, Freehold. Triple Play Toy, Comic Book, Sports Card, Memorabilia & Collectible Show. Raceway Mall, 3710 Route 9 (across from Freehold Racetrack). SH: mall hrs., T: 100-8', A: free. F & B Sport Cards, Inc., Ferdinand Parascandolo, 482 Retford Ave., SI, NY 10306. PH: 718-667-9588 or 967-9172.

Oct 21-22 2000 NJ, Atlantic City. Holiday Mega Fair. Convention Center, One Ocean Way. SH: Sat. 10am-8pm, Sun. 10am-5pm. Brimfield Assoc., Inc., PO Box 1800, Ocean City, NJ 08226. PH: 609-926-1800.

Oct 27-29 2000 NJ, East Brunswick. Triple Play Sports Card, Memorabilia, Beanie Baby, Comic Book & Collectible Toy Show. Brunswick Square Mall, 755 Rt. 18. SH: mall hrs., T: 65-8', A: free. F & B Promos., Ferdinand Parascandolo, 482 Retford Ave., SI, NY 10306. PH: 718-667-9588 or 967-9172.

Nov 5 2000 NJ, Wayne. Toy & Collectibles Show. Co. #1 Firemen's Convention Ctr., 1 Parish Dr. off Rt. 23 North at Lincoln Park Exit. SH: 9am-3pm, T: 100-6', A: free. Phil De Mario, PO Box 4094, Wayne, NJ 07474. PH: 973-667-2112.

Dec 3 2000 NJ, Wayne. Toy & Collectibles Show. Co. #1 Firemen's Convention Ctr., 1 Parish Dr. off Rt. 23 North at Lincoln Park Exit. SH: 9am-3pm, T: 100-6', A: free. Phil De Mario, PO Box 4094, Wayne, NJ 07474. PH: 973-667-2112.

NEW MEXICO

Mar 4 2000 NM, Albuquerque. Route 66 Antique Toy, Doll & Collectible Show. State Fair Creative Arts Center Bldg. SH: 9am-3pm, A: $2.50, under 10 free. Jim Gallegos, PO Box 15414, Rio Rancho, NM 87174. PH: 505-892-8848.

May 20 2000 NM, Albuquerque. Route 66 Antique Toy, Doll & Collectible Show. State Fair Creative Arts Center Bldg. SH: 9am-3pm, A: $2.50, under 10 free. Jim Gallegos, PO Box 15414, Rio Rancho, NM 87174. PH: 505-892-8848.

Nov 4 2000 NM, Albuquerque. Route 66 Antique Toy, Doll & Collectible Show. State Fair Creative Arts Center Bldg. SH: 9am-3pm, A: $2.50, under 10 free. Jim Gallegos, PO Box 15414, Rio Rancho, NM 87174. PH: 505-892-8848.

NEW YORK

Jan 2 2000 NY, Hudson. Philmont Mountain Toy & Railroad Club Toy & Train Swap Meet. American Legion, 7 Fairview Ave. SH: 9am-2pm, A: $3. Rick Washburn, 12 Hudson St., Hudson, NY 12534. PH: 518-828-7902.

Jan 2 2000 NY, Lindenhurst. Northern Spur Train & Diecast, Hess Show. Knights of Columbus Hall, 400 S. Broadway. SH: 8:30am-1pm, T: 105, A: $3., children under 12 free. Carmelo Sancetta, PO Box 1286-M, Bay Shore, NY 11706. PH: 631-666-6855.

Jan 9 2000 NY, Elmont-LI. Model Train & Toy Show. St. Vincent De Paul School Auditorium, 1500 DePaul. SH: 10am-3pm. Frank Deorio, 1500 DePaul St., Elmont, NY 11003. PH: 516-352-2127.

Jan 16 2000 NY, Freeport. L.I. Comic Book &

Collector's Market Convention. Recreation Ctr., 130 E. Merrick Rd. SH: 10am-5pm, T: 45, A: free. Cosmic Comics, Ken Diamond, 246 Merrick Rd., Oceanside, NY 11572. PH: 516-763-1133.

Jan 22 2000 NY, Manhattan. Big Apple Toy & Comic Book Convention. St. Paul Church Auditorium, 9th Ave. & 60th St. SH: Sat. 10am-6pm. Big Apple Conventions, 74-05 Metropolitan Ave., Middle Village, NY 11379. PH/FAX: 718-326-2713.

Jan 22 2000 NY, Binghamton. Model Car Swap Meets. Comfort Inn, 1156 Upper Front St., easy off easy on Exit 6 Rt. 81. SH: 9am-3pm, A: free. Butch Somers, PH: 607-722-2716.

Jan 23 2000 NY, Patchogue. Toyworks 2000. K of C, 9-11 Railroad Ave. SH: 10am-4pm, T: 75, A: $3., under 12 free. Larry LaSpisa, PO Box 793, Patchogue, NY 11772. PH: 516-758-5600.

Jan 30 2000 NY, Freeport. Toy Memories Antique Toy Show. Recreation Ctr., 130 E. Merrick Rd. SH: 10am-3pm, T: 150, A: $5. Guy De Marco, PO Box 224, West Hempstead, NY 11552. PH: 516-593-8198.

Feb 5-6 2000 NY, Stony Brook. Greenberg's Great Train & Collectible Toy Show. State Univ. of NY, Sports Complex. SH: Sat. 11am-5pm, Sun. 11am-4pm, A: $6., $2. ages 6-12, under 6 free. Greenberg Shows, 7566 Main St., Sykesville, MD 21784. PH: 410-795-7447.

Feb 6 2000 NY, Syracuse. Collectorsfest. State Fairgrounds, Horticutural Bldg., State Fair Blvd., Rt. 690, Exit 7. SH: 10am-4pm, T: 200-8', A: $3., under 8 free. Central NY Promos., Lyn Lake, 35 Hubbard St. Ste. 1, Cortland, NY 13045. PH: 607-753-8580 eves.

Feb 13-17 2000 NY, New York. Int'l. Model Hobby Manufacturers Assoc. MIAA Pavilion at American Int'l. Toy Fair. Jacob Javits Conv. Ctr. Offinger Management Co., 1100-H Brandywine Blvd., Zanesville, OH 43702. PH: 740-452-4541 or FAX: 740-452-2552.

Feb 13 2000 NY, Franklin Square-LI. Model Train & Toy Show. VFW Hall, 68 Lincoln Rd. SH: 9am-1pm. Rae Romano, PH: 516-486-6658.

Feb 13 2000 NY, Freeport. L.I. Comic Book & Collector's Market Convention. Recreation Ctr., 130 E. Merrick Rd. SH: 10am-5pm, T: 45, A: free. Cosmic Comics, Ken Diamond, 246 Merrick Rd., Oceanside, NY 11572. PH: 516-763-1133.

Feb 20 2000 NY, Lindenhurst. Northern Spur Train & Diecast, Hess Show. Knights of Columbus Hall, 400 S. Broadway. SH: 8:30am-1pm, T: 105, A: $3., children under 12 free. Carmelo Sancetta, PO Box

1286-M, Bay Shore, NY 11706. PH: 631-666-6855.

Feb 26 2000 NY, Rochester. 12th Annual Toy & Collectible Show. Irondequoit High School, 260 Cooper. SH: 10am-4pm, A: $1. Tim Mabb, 13 Wysteria Ln., Rochester, NY 14617. PH: 716-342-6343 or 544-6046.

Mar 4 2000 NY, Albany. 29th Annual Toy Show. Polish Community Ctr., Washington Ave. Extension. SH: 9am-2pm, A: $3., under 12 free with adult. N.T.C., PO Box 2, Medusa, NY 12120. PH: 518-966-5239 eves.

Mar 12 2000 NY, Rochester. Toy & Collectible Show. Village Gate Square Mall, 274 N. Goodman St. SH: 10am-4pm, T: 150, A: free. Thomas Caulkins, Sr., 274 N. Goodman St., Rochester, NY 14607. PH: 716-442-5700.

Mar 19 2000 NY, Lindenhurst. Northern Spur Train & Diecast, Hess Show. Knights of Columbus Hall, 400 S. Broadway. SH: 8:30am-1pm, T: 105, A: $3., children under 12 free. Carmelo Sancetta, PO Box 1286-M, Bay Shore, NY 11706. PH: 631-666-6855.

Mar 26 2000 NY, Franklin Square-LI. Model Train & Toy Show. VFW Hall, 68 Lincoln Rd. SH: 9am-1pm. Rae Romano, PH: 516-486-6658.

Apr 1 2000 NY, New Hartford. Wonderful World Of OZ Show. First United Methodist Church, 105 Genesee St. SH: 10am-4pm, T: 65, A: $3.50. Mary Polera, 1236 Hammond Ave., Utica, NY 13501. PH: 315-735-5628.

Apr 8 2000 NY, Syracuse. A Century Of Dolls 1900-2000. Bellevue Heights United Methodist Church, 2112 S. Geddes St. SH: 10am-4pm, A: $3.50, $.75 children 12 & under. Peter Mylon, 601 Bradford Pky., Syracuse, NY 13224. PH: 315-446-6246.

Apr 9 2000 NY, Elmont-LI. Model Train & Toy Show. St. Vincent DePaul School Auditorium, 1500 DePaul. SH: 10am-3pm. Frank Deorio, 1500 DePaul St., Elmont, NY 11003. PH: 516-352-2127.

Apr 9 2000 NY, Freeport. L.I. Comic Book & Collector's Market Convention. Recreation Ctr., 130 E. Merrick Rd. SH: 10am-5pm, T: 45, A: free. Cosmic Comics, Ken Diamond, 246 Merrick Rd., Oceanside, NY 11572. PH: 516-763-1133.

Apr 15 2000 NY, Binghamton. Model Car Swap Meets. Comfort Inn, 1156 Upper Front St., easy off easy on Exit 6 Rt. 81. SH: 9am-3pm, A: free. Butch Somers, PH: 607-722-2716.

Apr 16 2000 NY, Syracuse. Collectorsfest. State Fairgrounds, Horticutural Bldg., State Fair Blvd., Rt. 690, Exit 7. SH: 10am-4pm, T: 200-0', A: $0., under 8 free. Central NY Promos., Lyn Lake, 35 Hubbard St. Ste. 1, Cortland, NY 13045. PH: 607-753-8580 eves.

Apr 29 2000 NY, New York. Barbie Doll & Fashion Doll Show. Holiday Inn Rockville Centre, 173 Sunrise Hwy. SH: 10am-3pm, A: $5., $2. under 12. Marl, PH: 941-751-6275 or Joe, PH: 323-953-6490.

May 7 2000 NY, Freeport. L.I. Comic Book & Collector's Market Convention. Recreation Ctr., 130 E. Merrick Rd. SH: 10am-5pm, T: 45, A: free. Cosmic Comics, Ken Diamond, 246 Merrick Rd., Oceanside, NY 11572. PH: 516-763-1133.

May 28 2000 NY, Franklin Square-LI. Model Train & Toy Show. VFW Hall, 68 Lincoln Rd. SH: 9am-1pm. Rae Romano, PH: 516-486-6658.

Jun 4 2000 NY, Lindenhurst. Northern Spur Train & Diecast, Hess Show. Knights of Columbus Hall, 400 S. Broadway. SH: 8:30am-1pm, T: 105, A: $3., children under 12 free. Carmelo Sancetta, PO Box 1286-M, Bay Shore, NY 11706. PH: 631-666-6855.

Jun 11 2000 NY, Freeport. L.I. Comic Book & Collector's Market Convention. Recreation

Ctr., 130 E. Merrick Rd. SH: 10am-5pm, T: 45, A: free. Cosmic Comics, Ken Diamond, 246 Merrick Rd., Oceanside, NY 11572. PH: 516-763-1133.

Jun 25 2000 NY, Franklin Square-LI. Model Train & Toy Show. VFW Hall, 68 Lincoln Rd. SH: 9am-1pm. Rae Romano, PH: 516-486-6658.

Jul 15 2000 NY, Binghamton. Model Car Swap Meets. Comfort Inn, 1156 Upper Front St., easy off easy on Exit 6 Rt. 81. SH: 9am-3pm, A: free. Butch Somers, PH: 607-722-2716.

Aug 6 2000 NY, Elmont-LI. Model Train & Toy Show. St. Vincent DePaul School Auditorium, 1500 DePaul. SH: 10am-3pm. Frank Deorio, 1500 DePaul St., Elmont, NY 11003. PH: 516-352-2127.

Aug 12-13 2000 NY, Rochester. 10th Annual National Toy Truck N' Construction Show. Dome Ctr. PH: 800-533-8293.

Aug 13 2000 NY, Franklin Square-LI. Model Train & Toy Show. VFW Hall, 68 Lincoln Rd. SH: 9am-1pm. Rae Romano, PH: 516-486-6658.

Sep 17 2000 NY, Freeport. L.I. Comic Book & Collector's Market Convention. Recreation Ctr., 130 E. Merrick Rd. SH: 10am-5pm, T: 45, A: free. Cosmic Comics, Ken Diamond, 246 Merrick Rd., Oceanside, NY 11572. PH: 516-763-1133.

Oct 21 2000 NY, Binghamton. Model Car Swap Meets. Comfort Inn, 1156 Upper Front St., easy off easy on Exit 6 Rt. 81. SH: 9am-3pm, A: free. Butch Somers, PH: 607-722-2716.

Oct 28 2000 NY, New York. Barbie Doll & Fashion Doll Show. Holiday Inn Rockville Centre, 173 Sunrise Hwy. SH: 10am-3pm, A: $5., $2. under 12. Marl, PH: 941-751-6275 or Joe, PH: 323-953-6490.

Oct 29 2000 NY, Syracuse. Collectorsfest. State Fairgrounds, Horticutural Bldg., State Fair Blvd., Rt. 690, Exit 7. SH: 10am-4pm, T: 200-8', A: $3., under 8 free. Central NY Promos., Lyn Lake, 35 Hubbard St. Ste. 1, Cortland, NY 13045. PH: 607-753-8580 eves.

Oct 29 2000 NY, Elmont-LI. Model Train & Toy Show. St. Vincent DePaul School Auditorium, 1500 DePaul. SH: 10am-3pm. Frank Deorio, 1500 DePaul St., Elmont, NY 11003. PH: 516-352-2127.

Nov 5 2000 NY, Lindenhurst. Northern Spur Train & Diecast, Hess Show. Knights of Columbus Hall, 400 S. Broadway. SH: 8:30am-1pm, T: 105, A: $3., children under 12 free. Carmelo Sancetta, PO Box 1286-M, Bay Shore, NY 11706. PH: 631-666-6855.

Nov 12 2000 NY, Freeport. L.I. Comic Book & Collector's Market Convention. Recreation Ctr., 130 E. Merrick Rd. SH: 10am-5pm, T: 45, A: free. Cosmic Comics, Ken Diamond, 246 Merrick Rd., Oceanside, NY 11572. PH: 516-763-1133.

Dec 3 2000 NY, Elmont-LI. Model Train & Toy Show. St. Vincent DePaul School Auditorium, 1500 DePaul. SH: 10am-3pm. Frank Deorio, 1500 DePaul St., Elmont, NY 11003. PH: 516-352-2127.

Dec 10 2000 NY, Freeport. L.I. Comic Book & Collector's Market Convention. Recreation Ctr., 130 E. Merrick Rd. SH: 10am-5pm, T: 45, A: free. Cosmic Comics, Ken Diamond, 246 Merrick Rd., Oceanside, NY 11572. PH: 516-763-1133.

NORTH CAROLINA

Jan 15-16 2000 NC, Raleigh. 33rd North State Toy Collectors Show. NC State Fairgrounds, 1025 Blueridge Rd. SH: Sat. 9am-5pm, Sun. 10am-4:30pm, T: sold out. Carolina Hobby Expo, PH: 704-786-8373.

Jan 22 2000 NC, Concord. 4th Annual Toy Vehicle Show. Nat'l. Guard Armory, Hwy. 49 & Old Charlotte Rd. SH: 9am-4pm, T: 100, A: $3. Carolina Hobby Expo, PH: 704-786-8373.

Jan 29-30 2000 NC, Charlotte. Toy, Train & Doll Show. Metrolina Expo Ctr., I-77, Exit 16-A. SH: Sat. 9am-5pm, Sun. 10am-4pm, T: 500, A: $5., under 12 free. Tri-City Shows, PO Box 825. Johnson City, TN 37605. PH/FAX: 888-955-TOYS.

Jan 29 2000 NC, Fayetteville. 31st Sandhills Toy & Hobby Show. Charlie Rose Expo Ctr., just off Hwy. 301 S. SH: 9am-4pm, T: 225, A: $4. Carolina Hobby Expo, PH: 704-786-8373.

Oct 7 2000 NC, Raleigh-Durham. Barbie Goes to...North Carolina Show. Sheraton Imperial Hotel Conf. Ctr., 4600 Emperor Blvd. SH: 10am-4pm, A: $5., $2. under 12. Marl, PH: 941-751-6275 or Joe, PH: 213-953-6490.

Oct 28-29 2000 NC, Charlotte. Toy, Train & Doll Show. Metrolina Expo Ctr., I-77, Exit 16-A. SH: Sat. 9am-5pm, Sun. 10am-4pm, T: 500, A: $5., under 12 free. Tri-City Shows, PO Box 825. Johnson City, TN 37605. PH/FAX: 888-955-TOYS.

NORTH DAKOTA

Jun 16-18 2000 ND, LaMoure. 15th Annual Farm Toy Show. PH: 800-533-8293.

OHIO

Jan 2 2000 OH, Bloomdale. 7th Annual Elmwood FFA & Alumni Farm Toy Show. Elmwood High School, 7650 Jerry City Rd. SH: 9am-3pm, A: $1.50, under 12 free with adult. Ed Feasel, PH: 419-655-3027 school or 447-4320 home.

Jan 7-9 2000 OH, Zanesville. Beanies, Sportscards, NASCAR & Collectibles Show. Colony Square Mall, 3575 Maple Ave. SH: Fri. & Sat. 10am-9pm, Sun. 12noon-6pm, T: 60-8', A: free. Jim Michaels, PO Box 8137, Zanesville, OH 43702. PH: 740-455-3121.

Jan 9 2000 OH, Columbus. Book & Paper Fair. Veterans Memorial Hall, 300 W. Broad St. SH: 10am-5pm, T: 325. Columbus Prods., Inc., PO Box 261016, Columbus, OH 43226. PH: 614-781-0070.

Jan 15 2000 OH, Celina. Benefit Race Card & Memorabilia Show. Eagle Lodge, 1400 State Rt. 703, E. SH: 10am-4pm, A: $2. Diane, PH: 419-394-7418 or Marge, PH: 419-586-5385.

Jan 22-23 2000 OH, Alliance. Beanie Babies, Sports Card, NASCAR & Collectibles Show. Carnation Mall. T: 50-8'. Paul Addams, 2812 Blenheim Ave., Alliance, OH 44601. PH: 330-823-6418 or 823-0398.

Jan 22-23 2000 OH, Columbus. Greenberg's Great Train & Collectible Toy Show. Franklin Cty. Veterans Memorial, 300 W. Broad St. SH: Sat. 11am-5pm, Sun. 11am-4pm, A: $6., $2. ages 6-12, under 6 free. Greenberg Shows, 7566 Main St., Sykesville, MD 21784. PH: 410-795-7447.

Jan 23 2000 OH, Eastlake. Railroad Show. Eastlake North H.S., 34041 Stevens Blvd. SH: 10am-2:30pm, A: $4. Bob Frieden, 9695 Chillicothe Rd., Kirtland, OH 44094. PH: 440-256-8141.

Jan 30 2000 OH, Cleveland-Akron-Medina. Toy Car Expo 2000. Medina Community Ctr., Cty. Fairgrounds, US 42. SH: 9:30am-3pm, T: 150. Brokaw's, PO Box 360033, Decatur, GA 30036. PH: 770-987-2773.

Jan 30 2000 OH, Mansfield. Toy & Collectible Show. Richland Co. Fairgrounds, Trimble Rd. Exit off US Rt. 30. SH: 10am-4pm, T: 175. Kevin Spore, PO Box 9014, Lexington, OH 44904. PH: 419-756-3904.

Feb 19-20 2000 OH, Niles. Greenberg's Great Train & Collectible Toy Show. Eastwood Expo Ctr., Eastwood Mall, 5555 Youngstown-Warren Rd. SH: Sat. 11am-5pm, Sun. 11am-4pm, A: $6., $2. ages 6-12, under 6 free. Greenberg Shows, 7566 Main St., Sykesville, MD 21784. PH: 410-795-7447.

Feb 27 2000 OH, Parma. Railroad Show.

Senior H.S., 6285 W. 54th St. SH: 10am-2:30pm, A: $4. Bob Frieden, 9695 Chillicothe Rd., Kirtland, OH 44094. PH: 440-256-8141.

Mar 5 2000 OH, Kirtland. Cleveland Old Toy Show. Lakeland College, I-90 & State Route 306. SH: 9am-2pm, A: $4. Bob Frieden, 9695 Chillicothe Rd., Kirtland, OH 44094. PH: 440-256-8141.

Mar 5 2000 OH, Columbus. Annual Doll Show. Aladdin Temple, 2850 Stelzer Rd. SH: 10am-4pm, A: $3. Vivian Ashbaugh, PO Box 465, Pataskala, OH 43062. PH: 740-587-4722.

Mar 11-12 2000 OH, Alliance. Beanie Babies, Sports Card, NASCAR & Collectibles Show. Carnation Mall. T: 50-8'. Paul Addams, 2812 Blenheim Ave., Alliance, OH 44601. PH: 330-823-6418 or 823-0398.

Mar 12 2000 OH, Findlay. Train Show & Swap Meet. High School, I-75, Exit 159, St. Rt. 224 E. to 1st light turn Rt. SH: 10am-4pm, A: $5., 12 & under free. Terry Oliver, 225 Mohawk Dr., Ottawa, OH 45875. PH: 419-523-4996 or Herb Corbet, PH: 419-523-6939.

Mar 12 2000 OH, Wooster. C J Trains-Spring Train & Toy Show. Black Tie Affair Party & Conference Ctr., N. side of Wooster, 50 Riffel Rd. SH: 10am-4pm, T: 8', A: $3., 12 & under free. Jon Ulbright, 941 Buchholz Dr., Wooster, OH 44691. PH: 330-262-7488 after 6pm.

Mar 17-19 2000 OH, Zanesville. Beanies, Sportscards, NASCAR & Collectibles Show. Colony Square Mall, 3575 Maple Ave. SH: Fri. & Sat. 10am-9pm, Sun. 12noon-6pm, T: 60-8', A: free. Jim Michaels, PO Box 8137, Zanesville, OH 43702. PH: 740-455-3121.

Mar 19 2000 OH, Kirtland. Champion Toy & Collectable Show. Euclid Beach Indoor Family Fun Center, 9193 Chillicothe Rd. (Rt. 306). SH: 10am-3pm, T: 100-8', A: $3., under 12 free. Bob & Marilyn Nicholas, 13896 Aquilla Rd., Burton, OH 44021. PH/FAX: 440-834-1220.

Mar 26 2000 OH, Mentor. Railroad Show. H.S., 6477 Center St. (State Rt. 615). SH: 10am-2:30pm, A: $4. Bob Frieden, 9695 Chillicothe Rd., Kirtland, OH 44094. PH: 440-256-8141.

Apr 9 2000 OH, North Ridgeville. Model Train Show. 7000 Pitts Blvd. SH: 10am-2:30pm, A: $4. Bob Frieden, 9695 Chillicothe Rd., Kirtland, OH 44094. PH: 440-256-8141.

Apr 9 2000 OH, Mansfield. Toy & Collectible Show. Richland Co. Fairgrounds, Trimble Rd. Exit off US Rt. 30. SH: 10am-4pm, T: 175. Kevin Spore, PO Box 9014, Lexington, OH 44904. PH: 419-756-3904.

May 5-6 2000 OH, Cambridge. Hopalong Cassidy Festival. Civic Ctr., Rt. 40 W. SH: 10am-5pm, T: 100, A: $5. Laura Bates, 6310 Friendship Dr., New Concord, OH 43725. PH: 740-826-4850.

May 6-7 2000 OH, Alliance. Beanie Babies, Sports Card, NASCAR & Collectibles Show. Carnation Mall. T: 50-8'. Paul Addams, 2812 Blenheim Ave., Alliance, OH 44601. PH: 330-823-6418 or 823-0398.

May 19-21 2000 OH, Zanesville. Beanies, Sportscards, NASCAR & Collectibles Show. Colony Square Mall, 3575 Maple Ave. SH: Fri. & Sat. 10am-9pm, Sun. 12noon-6pm, T: 60-8', A: free. Jim Michaels, PO Box 8137, Zanesville, OH 43702. PH: 740-455-3121.

Jul 22-23 2000 OH, Alliance. Beanie Babies, Sports Card, NASCAR & Collectibles Show. Carnation Mall. T: 50-8'. Paul Addams, 2812 Blenheim Ave., Alliance, OH 44601. PH: 330-823-6418 or 823-0398.

Jul 28-30 2000 OH, Zanesville. Beanies, Sportscards, NASCAR & Collectibles Show. Colony Square Mall, 3575 Maple Ave. SH: Fri. & Sat. 10am-9pm, Sun. 12noon-6pm, T: 60-8', A: free. Jim Michaels, PO Box 8137, Zanesville, OH 43702. PH: 740-455-3121.

Sep 3 2000 OH, Mansfield. Toy & Collectible Show. Richland Co. Fairgrounds, Trimble Rd. Exit off US Rt. 30. SH: 10am-4pm, T: 175. Kevin Spore, PO Box 9014, Lexington, OH 44904. PH: 419-756-3904.

Sep 9-10 2000 OH, Alliance. Beanie Babies, Sports Card, NASCAR & Collectibles Show. Carnation Mall. T: 50-8'. Paul Addams, 2812 Blenheim Ave., Alliance, OH 44601. PH: 330-823-6418 or 823-0398.

Oct 6-8 2000 OH, Zanesville. Beanies, Sportscards, NASCAR & Collectibles Show. Colony Square Mall, 3575 Maple Ave. SH: Fri. & Sat. 10am-9pm, Sun. 12noon-6pm, T: 60-8', A: free. Jim Michaels, PO Box 8137, Zanesville, OH 43702. PH: 740-455-3121.

Oct 28-29 2000 OH, Alliance. Beanie Babies, Sports Card, NASCAR & Collectibles Show. Carnation Mall. T: 50-8'. Paul Addams, 2812 Blenheim Ave., Alliance, OH 44601. PH: 330-823-6418 or 823-0398.

Nov 5 2000 OH, Mansfield. Toy & Collectible Show. Richland Co. Fairgrounds, Trimble Rd. Exit off US Rt. 30. SH: 10am-4pm, T: 175. Kevin Spore, PO Box 9014, Lexington, OH 44904. PH: 419-756-3904.

OKLAHOMA

Feb 26 2000 OK, Tulsa. Toy Cars & Auto Collectibles Show. Nat'l. Guard Armory, 3902 E. 15th. SH: 9am-4pm, T: 100, A: $1. Randy Smith, 8335 E. 14th, Tulsa, OK 74112. PH: 918-835-6074.

PENNSYLVANIA

Jan 2 2000 PA, Leesport. Old Toy & Collector Toy Show, Sports Cards & Racing Memorabilia. Farmers Market Social Hall, Rt. 61. SH: 8:30am-2pm, T: 150. Charles Gallagher, PH: 610-562-9404.

Jan 9 2000 PA, New Hope. Toy & Train Show. Eagle Fire Co., Rt. 202 & Sugan Rd. SH: 8am-12noon, A: $3. Fred Dauncey, 1443 Leonard St., S. Plainfield, NJ 07080. PH: 908-755-7989 or 0346.

Jan 9 2000 PA, Trevose. Antique & Collectible Doll Show. Radisson Hotel. SH: 10am-3pm, A: $5., $2. under 12 & over 65. PH/FAX: 718-428-0829.

Jan 15-16 2000 PA, Lebanon. Greenberg's Great Train & Collectible Toy Show. Valley Expo Ctr. at the Fairgrounds, 2120 Cornwall Rd. SH: Sat. 11am-5pm, Sun. 11am-4pm, A: $6., $2. ages 6-12, under 6 free. Greenberg Shows, 7566 Main St., Sykesville, MD 21784. PH: 410-795-7447.

Jan 30 2000 PA, Shrewsbury. Super Sunday Collectors Toy Show. Fire Hall. SH: 9am-1:30pm, T: 6', A: $2., under 12 free. Joe Golabiewski, PH: 410-592-5854 or Carl Daehnke, PH: 717-764-5411.

Feb 6 2000 PA, New Hope. Toy & Train Show. Eagle Fire Co., Rt. 202 & Sugan Rd. SH: 8am-12noon, A: $3. Fred Dauncey, 1443 Leonard St., S. Plainfield, NJ 07080. PH: 908-755-7989 or 0346.

Feb 13 2000 PA, Gilbertsville. Train-O-Rama & Toy Show. Fire House, Rt. 73 (E. of Rt. 100). SH: 9am-2pm. Mary Preudhomme, 233 Long Lane Rd., Boyertown, PA 19512. PH: 610-367-7857.

Feb 20 2000 PA, Allentown. Greater Northeast Doll & Teddy Bear Spring Expo Show. Days Inn Conference Ctr., 1151 Bulldog Dr. (intersection of 309N & Rt. 22). SH: 10am-4pm, A: $4., $1.50 children. PH: 570-620-2422.

Feb 26-27 2000 PA, Monroeville. Greenberg's Great Train & Collectible Toy Show. Pittsburgh ExpoMart, 105 Mall Boulevard. SH: Sat. 11am-5pm, Sun. 11am-4pm, A: $6., $2. ages 6-12, under 6 free. Greenberg Shows, 7566 Main St., Sykesville, MD 21784. PH: 410-795-7447.

Feb 27 2000 PA, Scotland. Train, Toy & Doll Show. Community Ctr., 3832 Main St. SH: 9am-3pm, T: 87, A: $2., under 12 free. Bill Robinson, 5678 Philadelphia Ave., Chambersburg, PA 17201. PH: 717-264-3081.

Mar 5 2000 PA, New Hope. Toy & Train Show. Eagle Fire Co., Rt. 202 & Sugan Rd. SH: 8am-12noon, A: $3. Fred Dauncey, 1443 Leonard St., S. Plainfield, NJ 07080. PH: 908-755-7989 or 0346.

Mar 5 2000 PA, Leesport. Old

Toy & Collector Toy Show, Sports Cards & Racing Memorabilia. Farmers Market Social Hall, Rt. 61. SH: 8:30am-2pm, T: 150. Charles Gallagher, PH: 610-562-9404.

Mar 19 2000 PA, Gilbertsville. Train Show. Firehouse, Rt. 73, 1 mi. E. of Rt. 100. SH: 9am-2pm, T: 200, A: $3., under 12 free. PH: 215-657-2477.

Apr 2 2000 PA, Hanover. Annual Train Show. Parkville Fire Hall, Rt. 94. SH: 9am-?, T: 100, A: $4. Ron Borsella, RD 2, Box 2478, Glenville, PA 17329. PH: 717-235-0640.

Apr 9 2000 PA, New Hope. Toy & Train Show. Eagle Fire Co., Rt. 202 & Sugan Rd. SH: 8am-12noon, A: $3. Fred Dauncey, 1443 Leonard St., S. Plainfield, NJ 07080. PH: 908-755-7989 or 0346.

Apr 16 2000 PA, Leesport. Old Toy & Collector Toy Show, Sports Cards & Racing Memorabilia. Farmers Market Social Hall, Rt. 61. SH: 8:30am-2pm, T: 150. Charles Gallagher, PH: 610-562-9404.

May 7 2000 PA, New Hope. Toy & Train Show. Eagle Fire Co., Rt. 202 & Sugan Rd. SH: 8am-12noon, A: $3. Fred Dauncey, 1443 Leonard St., S. Plainfield, NJ 07080. PH: 908-755-7989 or 0346.

May 21 2000 PA, New Hope. Doll Show. Eagle Fire Co., Rt. 202 & Sugan Rd. SH: 10am-3pm, A: $3., under 12 free. PH: 215-657-2477.

Jun 4 2000 PA, New Hope. Toy &

Train Show. Eagle Fire Co., Rt. 202 & Sugan Rd. SH: 8am-12noon, A: $3. Fred Dauncey, 1443 Leonard St., S. Plainfield, NJ 07080. PH: 908-755-7989 or 0346.

Jul 2 2000 PA, Leesport. Old Toy & Collector Toy Show, Sports Cards & Racing Memorabilia. Farmers Market Social Hall, Rt. 61. SH: 8:30am-2pm, T: 150. Charles Gallagher, PH: 610-562-9404.

Jul 9 2000 PA, New Hope. Toy & Train Show. Eagle Fire Co., Rt. 202 & Sugan Rd. SH: 8am-12noon, A: $3. Fred Dauncey, 1443 Leonard St., S. Plainfield, NJ 07080. PH: 908-755-7989 or 0346.

Aug 20 2000 PA, Gilbertsville. Train-O-Rama & Toy Show. Fire House, Rt. 73 (E. of Rt. 100). SH: 9am-2pm. Mary Preudhomme, 233 Long Lane Rd., Boyertown, PA 19512. PH: 610-367-7857.

Sep 3 2000 PA, New Hope. Toy & Train Show. Eagle Fire Co., Rt. 202 & Sugan Rd. SH: 8am-12noon, A: $3. Fred Dauncey, 1443 Leonard St., S. Plainfield, NJ 07080. PH: 908-755-7989 or 0346.

Sep 3 2000 PA, Leesport. Old Toy & Collector Toy Show, Sports Cards & Racing Memorabilia. Farmers Market Social Hall, Rt. 61. SH: 8:30am-2pm, T: 150. Charles Gallagher, PH: 610-562-9404.

Oct 1 2000 PA, New Hope. Toy & Train Show. Eagle Fire Co., Rt. 202 & Sugan Rd. SH:

8am-12noon, A: $3. Fred Dauncey, 1443 Leonard St., S. Plainfield, NJ 07080. PH: 908-755-7989 or 0346.

Nov 5 2000 PA, New Hope. Toy & Train Show. Eagle Fire Co., Rt. 202 & Sugan Rd. SH: 8am-12noon, A: $3. Fred Dauncey, 1443 Leonard St., S. Plainfield, NJ 07080. PH: 908-755-7989 or 0346.

Nov 5 2000 PA, Leesport. Old Toy & Collector Toy Show, Sports Cards & Racing Memorabilia. Farmers Market Social Hall, Rt. 61. SH: 8:30am-2pm, T: 150. Charles Gallagher, PH: 610-562-9404.

Dec 3 2000 PA, Leesport. Old Toy & Collector Toy Show, Sports Cards & Racing Memorabilia. Farmers Market Social Hall, Rt. 61. SH: 8:30am-2pm, T: 150. Charles Gallagher, PH: 610-562-9404.

Dec 10 2000 PA, New Hope. Toy & Train Show. Eagle Fire Co., Rt. 202 & Sugan Rd. SH: 8am-12noon, A: $3. Fred Dauncey, 1443 Leonard St., S. Plainfield, NJ 07080. PH: 908-755-7989 or 0346.

SOUTH DAKOTA

Feb 19-20 2000 SD, Sioux Falls. 19th Annual Greater Midwest Toy Show. Oaks Motel, Exit 81, I-29. SH: Sat. 9am-4:15pm, Sun. 9am-3:15pm, T: 240, A: $2.50. Glen Oldre, Box 277, Earlham, IA 50072. PH: 515-758-2725.

TENNESSEE

Jan 22-23 2000 TN, Johnson City-Kingsport-Bristol. Toy, Train & Doll Show. Appalachian Fairgrounds, I-181, Exit 42. SH: Sat. 9am-5pm, Sun. 10am-4pm, T: 300, A: $5., under 12 free. Tri-City Shows, PO Box 825. Johnson City, TN 37605. PH/FAX: 888-955-TOYS.

TEXAS

Jan 15 2000 TX, Waco. Wintertime Toy & Doll Show. General Exhibit Bldg., H.O.T. Fairgrounds, 4601 Bosque Blvd. SH: 10am-4pm, T: 300, A: $2.50, $.50 under 12. Productions Unlimited, 7334 N. May Ave., Oklahoma City, OK 73116. PH: 405-810-1010 or FAX: 405-340-3770.

Jan 27 1999 TX, Mesquite. Toy & Doll Show. Convention Ctr., 1700 Rodeo Dr. SH: 10am-4pm, A: $3., $1. under 12. Productions Unlimited, 7334 N. May Ave., Oklahoma City, OK 73116. PH: 405-810-1010 or FAX: 405-340-3770.

Jan 29 2000 TX, Corpus Christi. Jean Huff Doll & Toy Show. Bayfront Plaza Convention Center, Shoreline Dr. SH: 9am-4pm. Jean Huff, Claud Huff, 24779 County Rd. 11C, Mathis, TX 78368. PH: 361-547-3757.

Feb 5 2000 TX, Austin. Winter Doll & Toy Show. Palmer Auditorium Lower Level, South First & Riverside. SH: 9am-4pm. Jean Huff, Claud Huff, 24779 County Rd. 11C, Mathis, TX 78368. PH: 361-

547-3757.

Feb 5-6 2000 TX, Houston. 4th Annual Celebrity Autograph Collector's Show. Sheraton Brookhollow, 3000 N. Loop West (Hwy. 290 & 610 Loop). SH: Sat. & Sun. 10am-5pm. Nolan or Wendi Sims, PO Box 899, Cypress, TX 77410. PH: 281-807-9797.

Feb 6 2000 TX, Houston. Toy Show. Sheraton Crown Hotel Conference Ctr., 15700 JFK Blvd. SH: 10am-3pm, A: $5., $2. under 12. Marl, PH: 941-751-6275 or Joe, PH: 323-953-6490.

Feb 12 2000 TX, New Braunfels. Hill Country Doll Show. Civic Ctr., 380 S. Seguin St. SH: 9am-4pm, A: $3., $1. children. Dorothy Sojourner, 625 Gruene River Dr., New Braunfels, TX 78132. PH: 830-625-3245 or 608-0308.

Feb 26 2000 TX, Gainesville. 14th Annual North TX Farm Toy Show. Civic Ctr., 311 S. Weaver. SH: 9am-4pm, A: $2., under 12 free with adult. Ed Pick, 504 CR 300, Muenster, TX 76252. PH: 940-759-2876.

Feb 26-27 2000 TX, Austin. Collectors Exposition. Palmer Auditorium, lower level, South First & Riverside. SH: Sat. 9am-6pm, Sun. 10am-4pm, T: 200, A: $3., under 12 free. Sally Wallace, 6702 Lexington Rd., Austin, TX 78757. PH: 512-454-9882.

Mar 12 2000 TX, Houston. 23rd Annual Doll Show. Radisson Hotel-Hobby Airport, 9100 Gulf Fwy. at the Airport Exit I-45 S. SH: 10am-5pm, A: $3., $1.50 children. Pat Black, PH: 713-864-5229 or Linda Sieck, PH: 713-283-5900 or FAX: 713-283-5999.

Mar 25 2000 TX, San Antonio. Hill Country Doll & Toy Show. Live Oak Civic Ctr., 8101 Pat Booker Rd. SH: 9am-4pm, A: $3., $1. children. Dorothy Sojourner, 625 Gruene River Dr., New Braunfels, TX 78132. PH: 830-625-3245 or 608-0308.

Apr 29-30 2000 TX, San Antonio. Collectors Exposition. Live Oak Civic Ctr. SH: Sat. 9am-6pm, Sun. 10am-4pm, T: 200, A: $3., under 12 free. Sally Wallace, 6702 Lexington Rd., Austin, TX 78757. PH: 512-454-9882.

Jun 17 2000 TX, Austin. Summer Doll & Toy Show. Palmer Auditorium Lower Level, South First & Riverside. SH: 9am-4pm. Jean Huff, Claud Huff, 24779 County Rd. 11C, Mathis, TX 78368. PH: 361-547-3757.

Jul 14-16 2000 TX, Dallas. Big-D Collectibles Show. Ramada Inn, Regal Row A & Hwy. 183. SH: Fri. 2pm-6pm, Sat. 10am-5pm, Sun. 10am-3pm, T: 200, A: Fri. $20., Sat. & Sun. $6. Don Maris, Box 200725, Arlington, TX 76006. PH: 817-261-8745.

Jul 22 2000 TX, Corpus Christi. Jean Huff 19th Annual Summer Doll & Toy Show. Bayfront Plaza Convention Center, Shoreline Dr. SH:

9am-4pm. Jean Huff, Claud Huff, 24779 County Rd. 11C, Mathis, TX 78368. PH: 361-547-3757.

Nov 18 2000 TX, Belton. Jean Huff Doll & Toy Show. Bell County Expo Ctr., Loop 121. SH: 9am-4pm. Jean Huff, Claud Huff, 24779 County Rd. 11C, Mathis, TX 78368. PH: 361-547-3757.

VERMONT

Feb 20 2000 VT, Bennington. Model Car & Toy Show. St. Francis Sacred Heart Parish Ctr., corner of Benmont Ave. & West. Main St. SH: 11am-4pm, A: $2., 12 & under free. Kevin Kees, Rt. 7A, Box 280A, Shaftsbury, VT 05262. PH: 802-447-7957.

VIRGINIA

Jan 8 2000 VA, McLean. Monthly Toy, Comic Book & CCG Show. Tysons Corner Holiday Inn, 1960 Chain Bridge Rd. SH: 10am-4pm, T: 80-6', A: $2., under 5 free. Capital Assoc., Inc., Jeff Rocen, 7952 Arden Ct., Vienna, VA 22027. PH: 703-912-1993.

Jan 8-9 2000 VA, Virginia Beach. Greenberg's Great Train & Collectible Toy Show. Pavilion & Convention Ctr., take I-64 to Rt. 44 E. Exit. SH: Sat. 11am-5pm, Sun. 11am-4pm, A: $6., $2. ages 6-12, under 6 free. Greenberg Shows, 7566 Main St., Sykesville, MD 21784. PH: 410-795-7447.

Jan 22-23 2000 VA, Chantilly. Greenberg's Great Train & Collectible Toy Show. Capital Expo Ctr., 4320 Chantilly Shopping Ctr. SH: Sat. 11am-5pm, Sun. 11am-4pm, A: $6., $2. ages 6-12, under 6 free. Greenberg Shows, 7566 Main St., Sykesville, MD 21784. PH: 410-795-7447.

Feb 6 2000 VA, McLean. Monthly Toy, Comic Book & CCG Show. Tysons Corner Holiday Inn, 1960 Chain Bridge Rd. SH: 10am-4pm, T: 80-6', A: $2., under 5 free. Capital Assoc., Inc., Jeff Rocen, 7952 Arden Ct., Vienna, VA 22027. PH: 703-912-1993.

Mar 5 2000 VA, McLean. Monthly Toy, Comic Book & CCG Show. Tysons Corner Holiday Inn, 1960 Chain Bridge Rd. SH: 10am-4pm, T: 80-6', A: $2., under 5 free. Capital Assoc., Inc., Jeff Rocen, 7952 Arden Ct., Vienna, VA 22027. PH: 703-912-1993.

Apr 1-2 2000 VA, Salem-Roanoke. Toy, Train & Doll Show. Civic Ctr., I-81, Exit 141. SH: Sat. 9am-5pm, Sun. 10am-4pm, T: 400, A: $5., under 12 free. Tri-City Shows, PO Box 825. Johnson City, TN 37605. PH/FAX: 888-955-TOYS.

Apr 2 2000 VA, Dunn Loring. Spring Show. Volunteer Fire House Community Hall, 2148 Gallows Rd. SH: 9am-2pm, A: $3., under 12 free. James William Brostrom, 6632 Cardinal Ln., Annandale, VA 22003.

Apr 9 2000 VA, McLean. Monthly Toy, Comic Book & CCG Show. Tysons Corner Holiday Inn, 1960 Chain Bridge Rd. SH: 10am-4pm, T: 80-6', A: $2., under 5 free. Capital Assoc., Inc., Jeff Rocen, 7952 Arden Ct., Vienna, VA 22027. PH: 703-912-1993.

May 7 2000 VA, McLean. Monthly Toy, Comic Book & CCG Show. Tysons Corner Holiday Inn, 1960 Chain Bridge Rd. SH: 10am-4pm, T: 80-6', A: $2., under 5 free. Capital Assoc., Inc., Jeff Rocen, 7952 Arden Ct., Vienna, VA 22027. PH: 703-912-1993.

Jun 4 2000 VA, McLean. Monthly Toy, Comic Book & CCG Show. Tysons Corner Holiday Inn, 1960 Chain Bridge Rd. SH: 10am-4pm, T: 80-6', A: $2., under 5 free. Capital Assoc., Inc., Jeff Rocen, 7952 Arden Ct., Vienna, VA 22027. PH: 703-912-1993.

Jul 9 2000 VA, McLean. Monthly Toy, Comic Book & CCG Show. Tysons Corner Holiday Inn, 1960 Chain Bridge Rd. SH: 10am-4pm, T: 80-6', A: $2., under 5 free.

Capital Assoc., Inc., Jeff Rocen, 7952 Arden Ct., Vienna, VA 22027. PH: 703-912-1993.

Aug 6 2000 VA, McLean. Monthly Toy, Comic Book & CCG Show. Tysons Corner Holiday Inn, 1960 Chain Bridge Rd. SH: 10am-4pm, T: 80-6', A: $2., under 5 free. Capital Assoc., Inc., Jeff Rocen, 7952 Arden Ct., Vienna, VA 22027. PH: 703-912-1993.

Sep 10 2000 VA, McLean. Monthly Toy, Comic Book & CCG Show. Tysons Corner Holiday Inn, 1960 Chain Bridge Rd. SH: 10am-4pm, T: 80-6', A: $2., under 5 free. Capital Assoc., Inc., Jeff Rocen, 7952 Arden Ct., Vienna, VA 22027. PH: 703-912-1993.

Sep 16 2000 VA, Mclean. Barbie Doll & Fashion Doll Show. Tysons West Park Hotel, 8401 Westpark Dr. SH: 10am-3pm, A: $5., $2. under 12. Marl, PH: 941-751-6275 or Joe, PH: 323-953-6490.

Oct 8 2000 VA, McLean. Monthly Toy, Comic Book & CCG Show. Tysons Corner Holiday Inn, 1960 Chain Bridge Rd. SH: 10am-4pm, T: 80-6', A: $2., under 5 free. Capital Assoc., Inc., Jeff Rocen, 7952 Arden Ct., Vienna, VA 22027. PH: 703-912-1993.

Oct 14-15 2000 VA, Salem-Roanoke. Toy, Train & Doll Show. Civic Ctr., I-81, Exit 141. SH: Sat. 9am-5pm, Sun. 10am-4pm, T: 400, A: $5., under 12 free. Tri-City Shows, PO Box 825. Johnson City, TN 37605. PH/FAX: 888-955-TOYS.

Nov 5 2000 VA, McLean. Monthly Toy, Comic Book & CCG Show. Tysons Corner Holiday Inn, 1960 Chain Bridge Rd. SH: 10am-4pm, T: 80-6', A: $2., under 5 free. Capital Assoc., Inc., Jeff Rocen, 7952 Arden Ct., Vienna, VA 22027. PH: 703-912-1993.

Dec 3 2000 VA, McLean. Monthly Toy, Comic Book & CCG Show. Tysons Corner Holiday Inn, 1960 Chain Bridge Rd. SH: 10am-4pm, T: 80-6', A: $2., under 5 free. Capital Assoc., Inc., Jeff Rocen, 7952 Arden Ct., Vienna, VA 22027. PH: 703-912-1993.

WASHINGTON

Jan 22 2000 WA, Fife. Western Harvest of Toys. Executive Inn Hotel. SH: 10am-4pm, T: 400, A: $3. Charlie Ostlund, 12415 51st Ct. E., Edgewood, WA 98372. PH: 253-863-6211 or Dan Marek, PH: 253-537-3172.

Mar 19 2000 WA, Pullman. Train Show & Swap. Beasley Performing Arts Coliseum, Stadium Way & Orchard Dr. SH: 10am-4pm, T: 100, A: $2. Ken Vogel, 400 E. Main St., Pullman, WA 99163. PH: 509-332-0505.

WEST VIRGINIA

Jun 16-17 2000 WV, Wheeling. 2nd Annual Marx Toy & Train Collectors National Conv. The Kruger Street Toy & Train Museum, 144 Kruger St. SH: Fri. 11am-8pm, Sat. 9am-3pm, T: 50-80. Allan Miller, 144 Kruger St., Wheeling, WV 26003. PH: 304-242-8133.

WISCONSIN

Jan 8 2000 WI, LaCrosse. Beanie Baby & Plush Toy Show. Shelby Mall, Mormon Coulee Rd. SH: 10am-4pm, A: free. MJ Productions, Mike Kulig, PH: 608-781-5150.

Jan 22 2000 WI, Appleton. Beanie Baby & Plush Toy Show. Valley Fair Mall, 2145 2 Memorial Dr. SH: 10am-5pm, A: free. MJ Productions, Mike Kulig, PH: 608-781-5150.

Jan 23 2000 WI, Milwaukee. Scale Auto, Hobby & Toy Swap Meet. Serb Hall, 5101 W. Oklahoma. SH: 10am-3pm, T: 250, A: $5. Unique Events, Jim Welytok, PH: 414-

246-7171.

Jan 23 2000 WI, Janesville. Doll, Toy & Bear Show. Holiday Inn Express, 3100 Wellington Pl. SH: 10am-4pm, T: 150, A: $3.50, $1.50 ages 6-12. Marge Hansen, N96W20235 County Line Rd., Meno. Falls, WI 53051. PH: 262-255-4465.

Jan 30 2000 WI, Milwaukee. Orphans In The Attic Doll, Toy & Bear Show. Serb Hall, 5101 W. Oklahoma Ave. SH: 10am-4pm, T: 140, A: $3.50, $1.50 ages 6-12. Marge Hansen, N96W20235 County Line Rd., Meno. Falls, WI 53051. PH: 262-255-4465.

Feb 6 2000 WI, Platteville. 9th Annual Model Car & Toy Show. Best Western Governor Dodge Motor Inn, 300 W. Hwy. 151. SH: 9am-3:30pm, A: $2., under 12 free with adult. Steve Swift, 320 Mound Ave., Belmont, WI 53510. PH: 608-762-5605 or Jeff Richardson, PH: 608-348-6400.

Apr 9 2000 WI, Milwaukee. Orphans In The Attic Doll, Toy & Bear Show. Serb Hall, 5101 W. Oklahoma Ave. SH: 10am-3pm, T: 100-140, A: $3.50, $1.50 ages 6-12. Marge Hansen, N96W20235 County Line Rd., Meno. Falls, WI 53051. PH: 262-255-4465.

Jun 11 2000 WI, Middleton. Orphans In The Attic Doll, Toy & Bear Show. Marriott-Madison West, 1313 John Q. Hammons Dr. SH: 10am-3pm, A: $3.50, $1.50 ages 6-12. Marge Hansen, N96W20235 County Line Rd., Meno. Falls, WI 53051. PH: 262-255-4465.

Sep 10 2000 WI, Milwaukee. Orphans In The Attic Doll, Toy & Bear Show. Serb Hall, 5101 W. Oklahoma Ave. SH: 10am-3pm, A: $3.50, $1.50 ages 6-12. Marge Hansen, N96W20235 County Line Rd., Meno. Falls, WI 53051. PH: 262-255-4465.

Nov 5 2000 WI, Middleton. Orphans In The Attic Doll, Toy & Bear Show. Marriott-Madison West, 1313 John Q. Hammons Dr. SH: 10am-3pm, A: $3.50, $1.50 ages 6-12. Marge Hansen, N96W20235 County Line Rd., Meno. Falls, WI 53051. PH: 262-255-4465.

Dec 3 2000 WI, Milwaukee. Orphans In The Attic Doll, Toy & Bear Show. Serb Hall, 5101 W. Oklahoma Ave. SH: 10am-3pm, A: $3.50, $1.50 ages 6-12. Marge Hansen, N96W20235 County Line Rd., Meno. Falls, WI 53051. PH: 262-255-4465.

CANADA

Jan 23 2000 ON, Cambridge. Millennium 2000 Toy Show. Waterloo Regional Police Assc. Inc., just 401 & Reg. Rd. 97. Kitchener-Waterloo. SH: 9:30am-3:30pm, T: 45. John Snyder & Randy Goudeseune, 168 Bloomingdale Rd., Kitchener ON N2K 1A9. PH: 519-742-6810 or 582-8767.

Jan 30 2000 ON, Mississauea. Annual Toy & Collectibles Show. Canadian German Club Hansa, 6650 Hurontario St. (1/4 mi. N. Hwy. 401). SH: 9:30am-2:30pm, T: 50. Claus Gunzel, 525 Highland Rd. W., Ste. 304, Kitchener, ON N2M 5P4. PH: 519-570-3120.

Mar 4-5 2000 ON, Nepean-Ottawa. 11th Annual Ottawa Train & Toy Show. Nepean Sports Plex, Salons A&B, 1701 Woodroffe Ave. (2 km S. of Hwy. 417). SH: Sat. 10am-5pm, Sun. 10am-4pm, T: 70. Toronto Show Promos., Frank Steele. Box 3A-10, Centreville, ON Canada K0K 1N0. PH: 613-378-0309.

Mar 5 2000 ON, Cambridge. Toy Show. Hespeler Arena, 640 Ellis Rd. SH: 10am-4pm, T: 83, A: $2., 12 & over. Brian Darling, 20 Harvest Ct., Kitchener, ON Canada N2P 1T3. PH: 519-748-6967.

Apr 16 2000 ON, Mississauga-Toronto. 16th Annual Toronto Toy Show. International Centre, 6900 Airport Rd. (.5 mi. N. of Pearson Airport). SH: 10am-4pm, T: 350. Toronto Show Promos., Doug Jarvis, Box 217, Grimsby, ON Canada L3M 4G3. PH: 905-945-2775.

COME ON AND DO THE *LOCOMOTION!*

Scenery for Model Railroads, Dioramas & Miniatures
3rd Edition
by Robert Schleicher
You'll learn the easiest and most effective methods for recreating the splendor of nature-but in miniature! Foolproof techniques are explained with easy-to-follow directions, step-by-step photographs and handy Reference Cards.
Softcover • 8-1/2 x 11 • 160 pages
120 b&w photos • 16-page color section
MRDM3 • $22.95

The HO Model Railroading Handbook
3rd Edition
by Robert Schleicher
Build exciting model railroad layouts with hot ideas, trends and products presented in an easy-to-follow, how-to style.   The author supplies all modelers, from beginners to experts, with the latest tips, tricks and techniques for building a new layout or refreshing an existing setup.
Softcover • 8-1/2 x 11 • 224 pages
250 b&w photos • 50 color photos
HOMR3 • $19.95

Large-Scale Model Railroading Handbook
by Robert Schleicher
You'll learn how-to from hands-on advice when it comes to building your track plans, buildings, and scenery. Also includes locomotive maintenance and upgrading tips.
Softcover • 8-1/4 x 10-7/8
224 pages • 16-page color section
LSMRH • $18.95

Standard Guide to Athearn Model Trains
by Tim Blaisdell and Ed Urmston Sr.
This book features more than 4,000 different models and a handy checklist format that will help you catalog your collection. Designed for both novices and professional collectors/dealers, this reliable guide will help you on your journey into this hot collectible field.
Softcover • 8-1/2 x 11 • 288 pages
420 b&w photos • 80 color photos
ACB1 • $24.95

Fun With Toy Trains
by Robert Schleicher
In addition to 24 exciting track plans, you will learn many facts on topics such as multiple train operation and how to use operating accessories. Whether you want to get more "play value" from your toy trains or learn the key considerations for selecting even more locomotives and cars for expanding your collection-it's all covered!
Softcover • 8-1/2 x 11 • 224 pages
160 b&w photos • 8-page color section
CMTH • $23.95

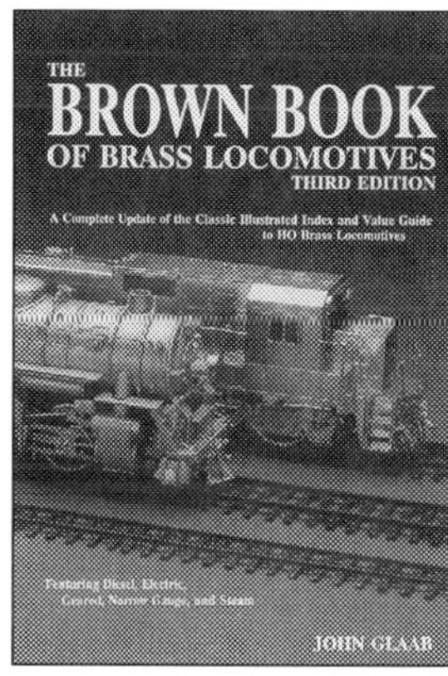

The Brown Book Of Brass Locomotives *3rd edition*
by John Glaab
Market prices for model brass locomotives of all types are in this updated edition.Models by class and type, manufacturer, and importer. Plus, you'll learn production runs as well as the original selling price. Illustrations help you identify numerous brass locomotives.
Softcover • 8-1/4 x 10-7/8 • 288 pages
BBBL3 • $24.95

Things you can do online...

search our classifieds for that missing item
for a job in the hobby field

order our latest books on collecting toys
a new subscription

renew your subscription to Toy Shop

find an answer to a nagging hobby question
the collectibles you want in our online classified ads

read all about your favorite collectibles

auction that item you don't need or find that elusive item

classified ads can be placed in Toy Shop
ads are also listed online

ToyShop
The Toy Collector's Marketplace

www.toyshopmag.com